Strangled

Identity, Status, Structure
and The Stranglers

Strangled

Identity, Status, Structure
and The Stranglers

Phil Knight

Winchester, UK
Washington, USA

First published by Zero Books, 2015
Zero Books is an imprint of John Hunt Publishing Ltd., Laurel House, Station Approach,
Alresford, Hants, SO24 9JH, UK
office1@jhpbooks.net
www.johnhuntpublishing.com
www.zero-books.net

For distributor details and how to order please visit the 'Ordering' section on our website.

Text copyright: Phil Knight 2014

ISBN: 978 1 78279 797 5

A CIP catalogue record for this book is available from the British Library.

Design: Lee Nash

Printed in the USA by Edwards Brothers Malloy

We operate a distinctive and ethical publishing philosophy in all
areas of our business, from our global network of authors to
production and worldwide distribution.

CONTENTS

Introduction

Picture for a moment a world in which the most significant practitioners of every particular musical style were written out of the history of that movement. For example, imagine The Beatles being excluded from the story of the Sixties beat boom; or Charlie Parker being mysteriously passed over in retrospectives of bebop; or King Tubby being omitted from narratives on the evolution of dub reggae. Such acts of neglect might seem unthinkable, and yet there is one genre whose self-appointed custodians do ensure the marginalisation of its greatest exponents, and that genre is punk.

For The Stranglers were the greatest punk band, not just in terms of commercial success, but also artistically. Though their peers often affected to shun them, it is remarkable how the group's bass-heavy sound and gnostic, alienated worldview percolated throughout the genre, until, a couple of years after the initial punk explosion, almost every other band had come to sound like them. The Stranglers were the eye of the hurricane, the black hole at the centre of the punk universe, a present absence without whom much of the history of punk seems inexplicable, yet is chronicled anyway.

So just why are The Stranglers marginalised in this way? The usual reasons given are the band's predilection for violence and misogyny, their hostile attitude to writers and journalists, their age and prior existence to punk's Year Zero, and their disinterest in attaining success in the USA. There is truth in all of these assertions, yet they only go so far. Go beyond the sexism'n'violence that marks out their early reputation and one finds that The Stranglers' music explores a multitude of often bizarre and seemingly unrelated subjects, such as UFOs, Japanese ritual suicide, the Cold War, European integration, genetic engineering, religion, conspiracy theories, the Vikings, the automisation of production, and the prophecies of Nostradamus.

What immediately becomes clear is that The Stranglers are a very difficult band to write about because they are very difficult to understand. The purpose of this book is therefore not to provide a comprehensive history of the group, or to chronicle the evolution of every one of their songs, but to lay down a theoretical basis from which their work as a whole can be understood. The book is constructed of two essays of unequal length, the first centred around singer and guitarist Hugh Cornwell, and the second concerning bass player and singer Jean Jacques Burnel. This may seem like an odd structure for a book, but, as will become apparent, an odd structure is perfectly appropriate when dealing with The Stranglers.

Some of the subject matter and issues uncovered by this investigation may prove unpalatable to some readers, especially those of a rationalist bent and/or a high social status (the two are of course related), and this will give an early clue as to why so many of our cultural guardians would like to pretend that The Stranglers had never existed.

Part I

Just Like Nothing On Earth

"Groups tend to reinforce their members' beliefs and expectations, and when this involves the paranormal, the effects can be insidious. If paranormal manifestations persist and grow, the usual rules of what is possible, reliable, etc. no longer apply. The trickster constellation strengthens. One consequence is the blurring of distinctions between subjective and objective, between imagination and reality. The problems are not limited to groups of 'marginals'. I have watched as medical doctors, high ranking military officers, university professors, and other normal, respectable people were overtaken by preposterous occult beliefs. The full force of this perhaps cannot be appreciated unless one experiences it first hand."
– George Hansen, "The Trickster And The Paranormal"

"I believed that if we thought about a UFO strongly enough, maybe we could evoke it."
– Hugh Cornwell, "The Stranglers: Song By Song"

* * *

On June 2 1973, the crypto-zoologist Frederick "Ted" Holiday partook in a strange ritual on the waters of Loch Ness. Holiday had long been interested in the folklore surrounding the monster that was alleged to reside in the depths of the Loch, and which had been increasingly sighted by both locals and tourists in the recent decades. His initial theory was that this "monster", far from being the reptilian creature of popular imagination, was an overgrown form of *tullimonstrum gregarium*, a species of prehistoric slug, but he had, during the late 1960s, become increasingly perplexed by the animal's apparent camera-shyness.

As outlined in books such as *The Dragon And The Disc*, he slowly became convinced that the Loch Ness Monster, along with other denizens of what he called "the phantom menagerie" such as the Yeti, the mystery big cats of the English home counties, and extra-terrestrials, were not real creatures, but what he called

2

"thoughtforms" – manifestations of the human collective unconscious that have a tendency to form when certain highly charged locations are visited by particularly sensitive individuals. Holiday, who claimed to have seen the monster on several occasions, regarded these manifestations as being irretrievably evil, the product of the more grotesque aspect of whatever unknown power organises the universe.

Holiday enlisted a Presbyterian priest by the name of Donald Omand to accompany him out onto the water to exorcise the loch. Although the exorcism passed off without apparent incident, within a few days Holiday and his accomplices were to encounter a bewildering array of bizarre phenomena, including mysterious flashing lights and sudden tornados that would shake the walls of their homes before abating in seconds. Holiday himself would come across one of the notorious "men in black" while attempting to investigate an alleged UFO landing site nearby. It was to be a fateful meeting – he would suffer a heart attack at exactly the same spot a year later.

Holiday was to die of a second heart attack in 1979, still firmly convinced that he had been the victim of the malign synchronicity of what he had termed, in his last book, *The Goblin Universe*. But what was the true nature of this strange, paranormal power that he thought he had identified? And who were going to be its next victims?

* * *

The events surrounding the recording of The Stranglers' fifth album, the conceptual *The Gospel According To The Men In Black* form one of the most extraordinary sagas in the history of popular music, and yet it is one that is little-known and rarely examined. It is a story that involves paradox, paranoia and the paranormal, and how these combined to derail the career of a band who, at the time, were considered to have the potential to be the most successful of their era. It is also a story of addiction, imprisonment, chronic misfortune, bizarre coincidences, and death. In order to gain some semblance of understanding of what happened, we will need to travel along some of the most neglected byways of Western thought and meet the most grotesque character in global folklore – The Trickster. Our primary guide will be the American author and parapsychologist George Hansen, who has done much to highlight how this unsavoury character, long thought to have disappeared as a primitive superstition, still operates in the margins of modern consciousness.

The Trickster archetype, whose very milieu is the marginal, the liminal, the disordered and the taboo, reveals much about the nature of The Stranglers, and particularly their singer and guitarist Hugh Cornwell. Unlike peers such as Paul Weller, Joe Strummer, John Lydon and Elvis Costello, Cornwell is something of a neglected figure nowadays, rarely spoken of in the same hagiographic terms. This is strange, as The Stranglers' frontman was once considered one of the most dangerous individuals in popular culture, being the only notable member of the punk scene that the British authorities considered worthy of imprisoning.

A similar taboo seems to surround The Stranglers themselves, who have been assiduously written out of the history of the punk and new wave movements. Thick historical volumes of the era barely reference them, except in the most curtly dismissive way. In 2013, a four-hour BBC television documentary on British punk didn't even once mention them by name. This extreme marginal-isation is usually explained "rationally" by the band's misogyny, violence, and tendency to make influential enemies, but, in an exhausted contemporary culture that compulsively seeks to reassess and rehabilitate even the most derided music of the past, it seems reasonable to suspect something deeper amiss.

Indeed, there is something unclean about The Stranglers. Even now, to think about them conjures a certain ominous dread.

Whereas the Sex Pistols and The Clash can be assimilated into healthy retrospectives of British pop, in which punk represents a mere burst of cultural vibrancy, there is something about The Stranglers that leaves the guardians of British popular culture feeling queasy. This pervasive aura of dread offers a clue both as to why they are so difficult to assimilate into accepted cultural narratives, and why they themselves became lured by the destructive chimera of the UFO phenomenon. Both of these tendencies suggest that the group were immersed in the phenomena of anti-structure, which is the natural domain of The Trickster.

The concept of anti-structure as its name suggests is intimately bound up in ideas of social structure. Its discoverer, the anthropologist Victor Turner, recognised that all social structures are created by the role-differentiation that an organised society requires. These variegated roles give definition and continuity to the lives of all the individuals within that society, and, most importantly, also denote the status relationships between those individuals. Structure by its very nature introduces hierarchy into human relations and thus some element of alienation and domination. By definition, status is structure, and a change in one will lead to a change in the other.

Within any society, the structure is pervasive but invisible, and Hansen perceptively likens it to a "spirit", in the paranormal sense of the word. Rather than society consisting, as we imagine, of discrete individuals and groups composed of discrete individuals, it is in fact composed of structures whose influence we generally choose not to acknowledge. These structures consist of boundaries within which the phenomena that we encounter in our daily lives are categorized, and these categories are normally composed of binary opposites, for example male-female, right-left, black-white, life-death, subject-object, etc. This binary classification system derives from the Aristotelian "law of the excluded middle", which lies at the heart of Western logic and rationality, and states that any observed object must be either "A" or "not A".

Anti-structure therefore refers to those collective phenomena that have a tendency to obscure or disrupt social structures by blurring or erasing boundaries, and by implication lowering or inverting social statuses. Such phenomena can include social stress and political disorder, altered states of consciousness (for example, those induced by psychoactive drugs), hoaxes and deception, crime, gender confusion, deviant sexuality, social marginalisation, travel, ritual magic and paranormal activity, amongst many others. Although these may at first appear as extremely disparate phenomena, Hansen notes that they often appear in clusters, and where one of them is apparent it is profitable to look for the others. For example, the period of political disorder prompted by the Vietnam War in the USA encompassed a whole host of anti-structural activities including the marginalisation of middle-class youth within the counter-culture, rampant drug experimentation, renewed interest in occultism (including attempts to levitate the Pentagon), a surge in paranormal activity, most notably in a further series of UFO "flaps", and a lowering of the status of the establishment with the disgracing of two presidents.

Indeed, anti-structure manifests itself in so many different ways that Hansen recommends we view it through the person-ified mythical archetype of The Trickster, a figure that is almost universal throughout the world's traditional folklores and mythologies, but is a marginal figure in the contemporary West. The Trickster represents a "constellation" of characteristics that manifest themselves when social structures are erased, suspended or inverted, and thus indicates the limits to Western logic, objectivity and rationality. In some cultures The Trickster is little more than a selfish buffoon, such as the Winnebago trickster Wakdjungkaga; in others he is a god, such as the Greek trickster god Hermes. They are associated with disruption, deception and sexual insatiability. In Greek mythology, Hermes, who is the half-brother of Apollo and Dionysus, is said to have assisted as a midwife at the birth of Dionysus, and therefore represents the passage between Apollonian order and Dionysian orgiastic excess. This is noteworthy because popular music, especially rock music, is erroneously identified as "Dionysian" when it would be more correct to describe it as Hermetic. Like Hermes, rock musicians help facilitate the social transition from order to disorder. Like Hermes, Wakdjungkaga, Loki and the Spirit Mercurius, they are anti-structural entities that blur boundaries and challenge existing structures. Unlike these trickster gods, however, they are rarely aware of the profound and disturbing consequences of their actions, because to be so would require an understanding of what these boundaries are ultimately erected to suppress, which is *the supernatural*. It is one of the keystones of Western rationality that the supernatural is marginalised through disbelief and ridicule, and though these are at least as effective in suppressing it as "primitive" proscriptions and taboos, they offer little defence on the occasions when it erupts into contemporary consciousness.

Hermes was also a messenger god who traveled between the Earth and the home of the gods on Mount Olympus; and, as a psychopomp, he accompanied the souls of the dead to the underworld. Here again, we see him crossing boundaries between binary opposites (heaven-earth, life-death). As with Eshu-Elegba, the trickster god of the Yoruba of West Africa, Hermes was explicitly identified with boundaries, known as *limen* in Greek, a word that is the root of our current term "liminal". Victor Turner stated that anti-structure was synonymous with liminality and also what he called "communitas", a term that refers to a period of (usually ritualised) temporary social leveling often seen in primitive cultures, in which the established order is set aside as a means of emphasizing the collective common humanity of the tribe. Again we can note that popular musicians are also perceived primarily as communicators – as the messengers of their generation – and that communitas is one of the unspoken goals of popular youth movements, as seen through the social leveling of the hippie, punk, and rave counter-cultures, with their abandonment of traditional social roles, erasure of previous identities, adoption of common modes of dress, and predilection for festivals and altered states of consciousness.

Hermes is also associated with the paranormal, as he was given the gift of prophecy by Zeus via the ability to interpret signs through divination, and the trickster scholar Jean Shinoda Bolen characterizes him as being the god of luck, coincidences and synchronicity. The term "hermeneutics", used to describe the interpretation of text, is derived from his name. He is also a thief and a deceiver, and the god of trickery in sexual seduction. If, in summary, we can therefore characterize Hermes as a disruptive, deceptive, libidinous messenger who erases boundaries through deliberate disruption, thereby unleashing the paranormal, we can see immediately that The Stranglers were an extremely hermetic band.

The idea of liminality had been previously introduced by the French anthropologist Arnold Van Gennep in his celebrated treatise "The Rites Of Passage", which was published at the turn of the twentieth century. Van Gennep had recognised that changes of individual social status within primitive groups had a cascading effect that rearranged the whole social order, and were thus perceived to be dangerous episodes in which supernatural forces may be tempted to intervene. These transitional, or liminal, periods, such as puberty, marriage, changes of leadership, or death, had to be protected by various ritual actions that warded off the supernatural and ensured the smooth passage from one status to the next for the individual(s) in question.

Van Gennep noted that initiations usually consisted of three stages; those of separation from the tribe, transition (the liminal stage), and re-incorporation. During the liminal stage, initiates were often physically separated from the rest of the populace, and this might include a period of wandering, sometimes involving altered states of consciousness ("vision quests"). Excluded from society, they might also be unbounded from accepted laws and customs, granting them license to attack or steal from the community without fear of correction. The initiates' liminal status outside the social structure makes them both sacred and dangerous, and they can therefore institute chaos. In this admixture of wandering, social marginality, altered states of consciousness, and anti-social, anti-structural behaviour we can again see a parallel with rock groups, with their endless rounds of touring, drug ingestion, sexual license, petty vandalism, and frequent attraction to religious and occult themes, much of which is tacitly excused by society in ways that it would be not be for ordinary citizens. It is entirely fitting that these groups often appear to be in a perpetual state of adolescence because they are, ultimately, enacting a perpetual initiation rite.

As we have seen, anti-structure gains its efficacy by disrupting structures that are composed of binary opposites. For each of the binary opposites that are used to classify our experience, one of the binary elements normally occupies a privileged position. As an example, if we were to take the binaries male-female, white-black, right-left, rich-poor, life-death and health-sickness, we can see that male, white, right, rich, life and health occupy the privileged position, and therefore are given a higher status than female, black, left, poor, death and sickness. It can be readily seen that these binaries have real implications for the way in which society is structured, and anti-structure generates its effects by equalising or inverting one or more of these binaries. The results can often appear disorientating and uncanny, especially to individuals who benefit from the higher status elements within these binaries.

This is why those in positions of authority are often hostile to anti-structure and communitas.

However, there is another way that anti-structure undermines binary opposites, and that is by the manner in which it locates what Victor Turner called a "betwixt and between" zone in the midst of the binary elements. Between white and black there is a grey area, and this is the area that the paranormal and super-natural inhabits. Between the life-death binary we find ghosts and spirits; between the heaven-earth binary we find angels, fairies and UFOs; between the man-beast binary we find yetis and werewolves; between the male-female binary we find the Native American *berdache*. So-called "primitives" fully under-stood that to subvert social structures carried the implicit danger of liberating the supernatural, and was therefore an extremely dangerous undertaking, and yet this understanding is absent in the modern, industrial West. Why should this be so?

The answer lies in an ongoing process that the father of sociology, Max Weber, called "the disenchantment of the world". Weber's thesis was that for several millennia mankind has been engaged in a process of ever-increasing sociological rationali-sation, which was initiated by the development of institutions such as government, the law, academia and corporate business, and then spread by their characteristic bureaucratizing effects throughout society. Although this process waxes and wanes in its intensity, its tendency is to rigidify hierarchical structures, increase codification, augment specialization, reduce opportu-nities for spontaneity, and enhance the individual's sense of alien-ation. Weber posited that one of the important side-effects of this rationalisation was a disenchanting effect – it tended to eliminate magic and the supernatural from the world, but George Hansen considers that this observation is slightly wrong. Rather than being totally eliminated, magic is merely marginalised; it is banished from the consciousness of elite groups, such as scien-tists and academics, but continues to pullulate in the social margins. In essence, elite groups have an aversion to the super-natural because firstly as primary products of, and agents for, rationalisation their status is dependent on the continuation of the process, and secondly they have a dim awareness that the supernatural is threatening to the social order in which they are comfortably nestled.

Weber noted another product of rationalisation: the routini-sation of charisma. In its "pure" form, charisma is experienced as a supernatural or superhuman quality; those who possess it recognise no existing authority or hierarchical structure as binding them or their followers. It is an anti-structural phenomenon, promising communitas to its disciples, and must continually prove itself in its ability to work miracles. Pure charisma is inherently unstable, and cannot support itself. Over time it attenuates and becomes traditionalized or routinized as lineage charisma (e.g. royal families), charisma of office (e.g. presidents and prime ministers) or manufactured charisma (e.g. the entertainment industry), among others. What exactly consti-tutes "the supernatural" is open to question. Certainly Hansen believes it consists of real numinous entities "out there" in the world. A more rationalist position would suggest that it is more likely to consist of projections of the unconscious mind, or other unexplored areas of the psyche. A middle position can be struck based on Carl Jung's idea of the "collective unconscious" in which common archetypes are interpreted across cultural groups. Whatever its true nature, the supernatural is experi-enced as real by those who cultivate it, or who chance across it, thus it has real social effects with real social consequences.

The propensity of certain individuals to experience paranormal or supernatural phenomena was addressed by the Tufts University psychiatrist Ernest Hartmann as part of his "mind boundary" theory. Hartmann suggested that individuals' mental characteristics can be divided into either "thick" or "thin" boundary types, which to a large extent reflect their social status, as though the propensity to rationalisation has an internal mental corollary. People whose minds have thick boundaries tend to appear to be solid, organised, perhaps even rigid, and have a propensity to follow thoughts through to completion. Thin boundary types are more fluid in their thoughts, are more prone to hypnosis, synesthesia and lucid dreaming, as well as being more likely to have had paranormal experiences.

Hartmann noted that thick boundary people tended to have stable marriages, and were likely to have successfully progressed through the career structures of bureaucratic organisations. Thin boundary types on the other hand were more likely to be divorced or separated, and were more likely to be in a creative field such as writing or music. Victor Turner drew an explicit parallel between liminality and creativity. The blurring and erasure of boundaries that accompanies anti-structure allows cultural elements to be disassembled and recombined in new and often unprecedented ways, from the playful to the grotesque. In return, creativity may not be without its dangers in increasing vulnerability to other anti-structural phenomena.

Finally, another route by which anti-structure can manifest in the modern rationalised world is through the practice of reflexivity. As Hansen makes clear, reflexivity is a seemingly innocuous activity that can have profoundly destabilising consequences. It refers to the concept of self-referentially applying the analysing criteria of any process to analyse the process itself. For example, a reflexive activity might involve psychiatrists studying psychiatrists, or anthropologists researching anthropologists. This is an almost certain way to make trouble, because it is likely to expose the unrecognised foundations upon which any discipline is built. One of the first academic settings in which reflexivity was utilised was during the early 1960s, in the field of ethnomethodology. The instigator of this new discipline, Harold Garfinkel, sought to uncover the hidden assumptions that underlay everyday interactions, and designed a number of uncomfortable "breaching" experiments in order to expose them, for example by asking his students to act like lodgers toward their parents, a role-playing exercise that generated considerable distress. One of Garfinkel's most intriguing experiments was to sociologically study sociologists, an enterprise that was poorly received by the sociologists themselves. The reason for their discomfort lay in the unacknowledged structural relationship that sociologists enjoy with those they study. As with ethnographers who study "primitive" tribes, sociologists, by the very act of observing rather than participating in the activities they study, are granted a higher status by the "objective" and "rational" nature of their research. For themselves to be studied sociologically was profoundly discomforting as it signified a loss of status, and indeed brought status issues to the fore. These experiments were quickly brought to a halt, and their results and implications obscured within the discipline.

Reflexivity is anti-structural as it exposes the arbitrary foundations on which status, and therefore structure, is built, and, as we shall see, one of the reasons The Stranglers caused so much trouble is because much of their behaviour was highly reflexive. They tended, whether deliberately or accidentally, to expose the hidden cultural assumptions by which the music industry and its denizens operate, thereby causing an acute discomfort that could only be attenuated by their marginalisation. One of the primary tensions within the music industry is that between structure and anti-structure, and as such it occupies an unusual position within contemporary rationalised society. It encourages anti-structural behaviour among its performers, and then seeks to profit from the resulting creativity. One of the by-products of this Faustian pact is levels of death and mental illness that, were they to have occurred in any other industry, would have resulted in it being shut down decades ago.

The structure of the music industry is complex and in many aspects unstable. The main productive units, the "artists", are for most of their careers engaged in intense competition for recognition and therefore status in what Nassim Nicholas Taleb would call a "tournament", in which a few winners garner extreme "scalable" rewards, a smaller number scrape a reasonable living, and the vast majority gain very little. Every artist, which may be a solo performer or a group, is part of a semi-autonomous structure that includes themselves and their managers, promoters, road crew and any other hangers-on which form their professional circle. If we ignore for the moment general social status differences based on race, gender, sexuality etc. and take an archetypal four-piece white, male rock group, we can define a hierarchical structure that goes, from highest status to lowest:

singer > guitarist > bassist > drummer.

The hierarchy can alternately be partitioned thus:

frontmen (singer + guitarist) > rhythm section (bassist + drummer).

This structure is reified on stage. The singer occupies the front centre of the stage, the guitarist is roughly a step back and to his right (because right has a higher status than left), the bassist is usually a few steps further back to the left, and the drummer is at the very back, obscured by at least one and sometimes all three of the other members. On one level this structure reflects the mind-body binary opposition, in which mind occupies the higher status (thus white collar > blue collar), with the singer doing the least (obvious) physical work, and the drummer doing the most. On another level it usually represents claims on charisma, with the creative pairing of singer and guitarist having greater access to the supernatural than the rhythm section in the "engine room" (a phrase suggestive of the bowels of a ship).

To the degree that each member of the band is happy with his position in the structure, the more stable the group will generally be. A stable structure can result in long, but often uninspired, careers, because the essence of creativity is in liminality. Fortunately, in most bands, status will always be contested in some way. Bassists and drummers may gain kudos by being especially skillful or charismatic, making them difficult to replace. This can be signified in many ways, such as the wearing of garish clothes, or being granted indulgent solos. Drummers can sit on raised podiums, and lavishly augment their kits. Raised status can result in being allowed to submit songs for recording, having a greater say in group decision making, gaining an increased proportion of the band's income, and any number of other small but significant ways.

Status competition between frontmen is usually far more acute. Guitarists may begin to write lyrics (usually the singer's province), and then start agitating to sing the occasional number. This threatens to blur a status boundary, and the singer may respond by hiring an additional guitarist to put the original one under pressure. Or he may agitate to have his own name foregrounded over the name of the band. Or he may attempt to split the band, often with the intention of re-forming it later without his over-ambitious sidekick. Whatever strategy he pursues, it is important to note that when a band splits due to stated *"irreconcilable artistic differences"*, this is usually a euphemism for unacceptable status claims.

Of course bands come in many structural forms, and there are a wealth of other factors that can influence status relationships, such as length of tenure, organisational skills, sibling rivalry etc., but a successful band is pulled between the antithetical poles of creativity and stability, and thus must chart a course between going off the rails (most often by drug abuse and internecine strife) and becoming bland and predictable. Over the long term, this is extremely difficult to achieve, not least because of the heavy toll exposure to anti-structure takes on individual members.

The wider music industry within which groups operate is dominated by the major record labels, which, in contrast to the artists they promote, are generally highly structured bureaucratic organisations. In many cases they are, or were, the sub-divisions of companies primarily engaged in the manufacture of electronics hardware, such as Electric & Musical Industries Ltd. (EMI), General Electric's Radio Corporation of America (RCA) and the Sony Corporation. For most of the history of post-war popular music, these have been stable, hierarchically structured businesses whose primary concerns have been the same as any other multinational corporation – self-perpetuation and growth through the ever-greater deployment of investment capital to enable increasing financial return. Major record labels are therefore innately resistant to anti-structure, despite their apparent dependence on it.

The major labels have a tendency to favour uncontroversial artists who are themselves sufficiently self-disciplined so as to be able to regularly deliver marketable "product" over extended careers. However, such artists tend to be poor at creating the media controversies that draw attention to the music scene as a whole, and so the industry tends to cultivate anti-structure, which is nervously nurtured at the fringes, and held in check both by its innately self-limiting nature, and by various checks and balances within the promotional system. Relations between record labels and recording artists are enabled and mediated by various intermediaries, most notably Artist & Repertoire (A&R) executives on behalf of the record companies, and managers on behalf of the artists themselves. These middle-men have gained an unsavoury reputation over the years, largely due to their proclivity for being dishonest, often callously so. On the other hand, they are often very creative, sometimes more so than the artists they represent. The reason both these cases may pertain is that these kinds of intermediary roles occupy a marginal position between the rigid structure of the business end of the industry, and the anti-structural domain of the recording artists. Managers and promoters tend therefore to either be fairly structured characters who have a reasonable tolerance for anti-structure (the honest ones, generally speaking), or anti-structural characters with at least some capability to endure structure (the dishonest ones, mostly).

These middle-men are often, for example, members of marginalised groups who have nevertheless had extensive experience within the structured realm of business. Some of the most famous managers within the industry have been homosexual, or Jewish, or a combination thereof. Malcolm McLaren, the manager of the Sex Pistols, and Bernie Rhodes, the manager of The Clash, were both Jewish and were both notorious tricksters. They were, by and large, more anti-structural than their charges. However, the strategy of keeping anti-structure at bay via the prophylactic of intermediaries is rarely completely successful for the major record companies. It is in the promotion of recording artists that the anti-structural elements of the music industry are let loose in the world, and yet paradoxically it is also within this sphere that anti-structure is limited and contained. Prior to today's internet media, promotional strategies began with the selection of an appropriate single for commercial release, followed by lobbying by the record company's promoters to have it played on national and commercial radio stations, the promulgation of poster and leaflet campaigns, and, where possible, the booking of television appearances for the artists themselves. Radio airplay, especially by the national BBC Radio 1 station, was the most important, and therefore the most controversial, aspect of any promotional campaign. The figures that notionally play, and therefore promote, the records on any radio station are the disc jockeys, who are themselves frequently anti-structural individuals, often unpleasantly so. Indeed the nature of their work, in which they converse with an imaginary audience that doesn't actually exist, necessitates a certain capacity to occlude reality. Such individuals were deemed unfit in themselves to select which records ought to be played and promoted by the hierarchically-minded BBC, and so bureaucratic playlist committees were formed under the rubric of maintaining quality standards, their real task being to filter out anti-structure. However, it is in the interface between record company promotional departments and media outlets that the seamy side of the industry is most likely to surface. Dubious practices can taint the industry as a whole, one such example being the payola scandal that engulfed BBC Radio 1 in the early 1970s, and which resulted in the imprisonment of the singer Janie Jones for supplying prostitutes in return for airplay.

Perhaps the most curious position in the media-promotional menagerie was that occupied by the music press. The weekly music papers of the time, notably the NME, Melody Maker, Sounds and Record Mirror, played an unusually significant role in the promulgation of the punk scene. This was largely due to the marginal socio-cultural position that punk initially occupied, where it was shunned by the "decent" majority, and because the polemical nature of the movement, with its critique of normative values, particularly lent itself to textual evaluation and theorising. Music writers are commonly known as "journalists", and this is misleading, as journalism generally only describes a part of their duties. They in fact blend the roles of journalist (investigating new trends, conducting interviews etc.), commentator (making broad-brush evaluations and predictions on the growth of any scene), and critic (reviewing records and concerts etc.). This blending of roles creates a certain ambiguity in the structural position of the music writer in regard to the music industry in general. He or she is part ethnologist moving amongst the strange tribes of youth culture, part anthropologist seeking predictable patterns within diverse trends, and part scientist sorting and labelling by defined value criteria.

These roles imply disengagement, and therefore, as the ethnomethodologists would suggest, higher status than the recording artists they write about. In fact, the status relationship between music journalists and performers is ambiguous and therefore somewhat awkward. In the early part of a recording artist's career, favourable treatment by the music press can be essential in gaining traction for their careers, and so music writers occupy a comparatively powerful position. Once a performer has maintained a long and profitable career however, their wealth and status may place them on a social level far higher than any journalist. Music writers can also be constrained by the subtle blackmail of record company A&R and promotional departments: harsh criticism of a label's favoured new artist may result in inhibited access to more established performers. The structure of the music press itself mirrored the "tournament" nature of the industry as a whole, with writers moving from self-published fanzines, to freelancing for the established papers, to hopefully "making their name" and gaining staff roles and editorships. This pervading sense of insecurity fed the notorious habit of journalists to move in herds, reflected in their tendency to engage in the "hype" of a new group, and then, as if in collective recognition of error, to subject the same unfortunates to a "backlash". Shrewd managers and promoters learned how to manipulate this phenomenon expertly.

The ambiguous relationship between music journalists and the artists they covered generated a number of taboos. One of these was the prohibition against writers becoming performers, and vice versa. At the margins, a journalist could perhaps moonlight in a minor role in an established group, joining it onstage occasionally to play saxophone, say; or a performer could submit an essay to a music paper on a matter he or she had particularly strong feelings about, but these would be hedged with allusions to eccentricity and indulgence. When, in 1979, JJ Burnel was asked by the NME to write an essay for them, the resulting piece, "Systems", was accompanied by a disclaimer from the editor that it had been written the previous year, and that Burnel had spent the intervening period pestering the paper to publish it. Clearly, the notion that musicians could write their own copy, or that journalists could perform their own music, dissolved the binary of performer and critic, and threatened the structure that maintained the music press. Therefore, although musicians and writers could wholeheartedly transfer from one role to the other (though this was rare enough), occupying both roles simultaneously was only permitted in the most frivolous circumstances.

A separate, but related taboo was the general journalistic prohibition against becoming a part of the story being covered. Journalists would occasionally follow a band on tour, and provide an intimate account of the inner world of traveling performers, as for example Lester Bangs did with The Clash, but within these reports the journalist's higher status as ethnographer was preserved. The tendency of The Stranglers to foreground the role of journalists through subjecting them to pranks and vendettas, thus enmeshing them within the narrative arc of the band themselves, had the effect of not just dangerously lowering the status of the individual writer involved, but of reducing the status of the profession in its entirety. To attack one music journalist was akin to attacking all of them, and the response of the music press to The Stranglers' agitations was as unanimous as it was venomous. The band were ostracised as though they were an infection. Although they tended to pick on the unfortunate, low-status junior reporters who were sent into the breach to interview them, it was usually the more status-conscious senior editorial staff who would take time out to condemn them. It is no surprise, for example, that Village Voice editor Robert Christgau, the self-styled "Dean of American Rock Critics" went out of his way to poison the band's reputation in America before they even arrived there.

However, the structural issue that The Stranglers exposed in their harassment of journalists was the key role that they played in the containment of anti-structure. As "neutral" observers and value-critics, music writers are the primary force for containing youth movements and preventing them getting out of control. They mainly do this simply by their disengaging role of naming and therefore classifying. The simple act of naming punk as "punk" was an essential first step in getting a cultural handle on this amorphous, ambiguous and threatening social trend. From there, antecedents could be compared and contrasted, "influences", whether musical, sartorial or philosophical could be identified and illuminated, and what initially appeared as a novel and unprecedented phenomenon could be seamlessly blended into the stream of post-war youth cults. Music writers are generally blind to this aspect of their work, because such an insight would require reflexivity. They are mainly focused on what they see as their role of generating excitement by discovering new bands, new scenes, and bringing them to public attention as breathlessly as possible. In fact their task is more subtle – they are like the control rods in a nuclear reactor, keeping the music scene cooking productively without the fissile material that powers it going into meltdown. The very real violence of The Stranglers was in itself antipathetic to this project – it blurred the boundary between performance and reality and opened up appalling possibilities within the culture at large. So where did their unprecedented antinomianism originate? To answer that question, we must journey to what was then one of the quietest and most peaceful cultural backwaters in Western Europe.

* * *

"In 1953 you had the so called 'rebels without a cause'. Students who revolted in Stockholm. That was the first revolt of the young rebels without a cause. They had everything. They were happy. They lived in a nice society. They lacked nothing. And suddenly, on New Year's Eve, they took to the streets and destroyed everything. No one could understand it."
– Jacques Ellul, "The Betrayal Of Technology"

The story of The Stranglers begins in the same place that the story of post-war Western youth culture begins: in Sweden. The riots that shocked post-war Sweden in fact began in 1948, with the *"påskkravallerna"*, the "Easter Riots" of students of Stockholm University and the Stockholm School of Economics, and continued to erupt throughout the following decade, often coinciding with significant dates in the Christian (and therefore pagan) calendar. To the Swedish establishment, the riots were a mystery; the nation had managed to avoid entanglement in the Second World War, existing awkwardly by trading with both Britain and Nazi Germany while being simultaneously blockaded by them both. As such the country had had to endure severe rationing in food and fuel, and then being accused of profiteering by the victorious Allies. Nevertheless the country had remained stable and peaceful in a Europe that had been subjected to catastrophic upheaval. Why here, of all places, would the young erupt into a seemingly unprovoked, purposeless frenzy?

This question would be asked again and again in the post-war West as country after country would experience sporadic, inexplicable youth uproars that would seem to erupt out of nowhere, and just as quickly dissipate. In fact, the appearance of stability in Sweden would offer a valuable clue to the origin of subsequent events – its experience of the War had, on the psychological level, been a long, nerve-wracking anticipation of disaster, with the expectation that either the Nazis or the Allies were preparing to invade (and with the latter having had concrete plans to do so). In essence, the Swedes had had an early taste of what would become the defining Cold War experience – that of everyday life continuing at a steady humdrum pace, while a devastating yet ineffable threat hovered above them. It would be this tension between a seemingly stable society in which material prosperity appeared to be continually on the increase, and the unbearable, intangible social pressures that lurked beneath, that would provoke the emergence of anti-structural phenomena throughout the West, the punk movement in Britain being the signal example.

By the 1970s Sweden was again occupying an ambivalent position within the political framework of Cold War Europe. Officially neutral, but living under the shadow of the Soviet presence in the nearby Baltic states, its defence forces were secretly being funded by the United States, who also based nuclear submarines off its west coast. Culturally it was considered, if at all, as a backwater, its indigenous form of socialist-leaning folk music, known as Progg, being unknown to the outside world. If it was renowned for anything, it was the "Swedish Sin", a catch-all term for its liberated attitude to sex, from the provision of sex education in schools to the rescinding of laws regulating pornography and sex clubs. It was a legend that contrasted strongly with the other myth that attached itself to the nation – that it was a place so drearily rational that it tended to engender rampant alcoholism and suicide.

And so it was in 1972 that the department of biochemistry at Lund University, located in the historic southern town that faced Copenhagen across the Øresund, welcomed a new postgraduate student from England. Hugh Cornwell, who had far from distinguished himself in gaining his degree from Bristol University, had inveigled himself into the venerable Scandinavian institution from contacts he had made during an earlier summer placement at the Lund University hospital, where he had served as a laboratory technician. Having no clear idea of his future, apart from a reluctance to return home from Bristol to London, he had followed the acid rainclouds across the North Sea in search of whatever opportunities might present themselves.

It was in Lund that the long, unlikely incubation of what would become The Stranglers began. Cornwell had been introduced to music at William Ellis Grammar School by his friend Richard Thompson, later of Fairport Convention renown, who had taught Cornwell to play bass and encouraged him to join his band, Emil And The Detectives. Despite this reasonably auspicious beginning however, there is no hint that Cornwell ever had any kind of long-term plan to make it in the music industry, let alone conceive a group that would become a byword for notoriety.

Born and raised in Tufnell Park, Cornwell, like all the members of The Stranglers, came from an ambivalent position within the class system, that betwixt and between zone occupied by the educated echelons of the upper working class and the lower tier of the middle class. Although comfortably far from the margins of society, it is nevertheless a liminal area whose progeny so often find themselves equipped with the intelligence and capabilities for social advance, but are bereft of the professional contacts and sense of social ease that makes such advance possible. They are, more often than not, middle class minds with working class insecurities, and consequently this frustration results in an innate tendency to provoke trouble. They are, in short, the very essence of anti-structure. As Cornwell was to tell Paul Du Noyer:

Britain is still class-ridden ... My parents were lower middle-class; my father worked hard all his life to bring up four kids and never really had the fruits of it. Even in retirement I think he thought, is that it? You work so hard to get a place big enough to bring up four kids, and then they all leave home and you're left with an empty house. What's all that about? I don't want to be in that situation.

It is therefore somehow appropriate that an individual with such an ambivalent social background should find himself in a nation that itself occupied an ambiguous position in global politics, and it was not long before Cornwell drifted into the seedy margins of Swedish life. His PhD research work at the University hospital was increasingly compromised by his involvement in the band Johnny Sox, which he had formed with Hans Wärmling, a multi-instrumentalist musician and composer who was working as a nurse at the university hospital, and a couple of American Vietnam War draft-dodgers, Gyrth Godwin and Chicago Mike, whose political refugee status enabled them to claim state benefits. This was not the first time that Sweden had quietly undermined an American war effort; during the Second World War, its runways had been notoriously full of interned US bomber aircraft.

The orderly nature of Swedish society clearly disturbed Cornwell at both a conscious and unconscious level, and Johnny Sox soon became a locus of antinomian activity. Both Cornwell and Godwin were farming cannabis at their respective residences, and the band itself was being part-financed by their friend Kai Hanssen, another draft-dodger, of Swedish ancestry, who was also a bank robber who had become Sweden's "No.1 Most Wanted Criminal" after shooting a security guard during a heist in Lund. In fact, the band paid for their PA system by setting up an interview between the fugitive Hanssen and an ambitious journalist, and funded their activities with cash that had been stolen during the robbery. As the serial numbers of the banknotes had been publicised, Johnny Sox used them to pay for fuel for their van, also provided by Hanssen, in the automatic telling machines installed in the petrol stations in the local area.

Cornwell's sojourn in Sweden appears to have influenced him in two ways. In the first instance, it shaped him as a musician. Although he wrote a few of the band's songs, his role in Johnny Sox was not a leading one. The main creative pairing was between Wärmling, who was by far the most experienced musician, and Godwin, whose spontaneity was the main source of inspiration. Although Cornwell was the guitarist, the curiously muted role that his playing occupied within the band's format would be carried over as they mutated into The Stranglers; his guitar would continue to remain somehow slightly in the background. Indeed, the unusual structure of The Stranglers' sound owes a great deal to the organic process by which it evolved seamlessly from that of a Scandinavian bar band.

Sweden would also, disastrously, influence Cornwell's attitude to authority. Being both a more coherent and familiar society than Britain, it was a country whose rules were more restrictive, and yet the greater level of social trust meant they were easier to break without discovery and subsequent punishment. He therefore began to adopt a habitual pattern of brinkmanship with authority that would prove to be ill-advised in respect to the far less naïve and forgiving forces of law and order back home. After having sheltered Hanssen after the robbery in Lund, Cornwell was paid a visit by armed policemen, and noted that the sergeant in charge wore *"a suit that smells of bureaucracy"*. The ease with which he distracted and dismissed these investigators was compounded by a somewhat bizarre event in Malmö, when he was smoking a chillum in the back seat of a car that was suddenly commandeered by a local policeman and driven around the block in a random steering and brake test. The policeman had failed to note the unusual smell emanating from the back seat, and had vacated the car without comment. These incidents appeared to demonstrate that the pettiness of the authorities was simply the reverse side of their dull-wittedness.

Nevertheless, Cornwell's extracurricular activities were undermining his ability to conduct his research work at the University hospital, and, becoming increasingly disillusioned with the sterile life of a biochemist, he asked his professor if he could be released from his duties. Having no more reason to remain where they were, Cornwell, Godwin, Chicago Mike and bassist Jan Knutsson decided to bring Johnny Sox to England. However, if the band had finished with Sweden, they would later discover, in a new guise, that Sweden had not finished with them.

The transition from Johnny Sox to The Stranglers was not marked by a clean break, but a period of osmosis, as, on arriving in England, established members left and new ones were recruited. Nevertheless the critical event that would provoke the formation of The Stranglers was the arrival of Brian Duffy at Gyrth Godwin's squat in Camden, in early 1974, in response to an advert placed in Melody Maker for a drummer to replace Chicago Mike, who had taken advantage of an amnesty for draft dodgers to return to the United States. Duffy had adopted the alias Jet Black, from the Gaelic word for black, *dubh*, which formed the root of his surname, and immediately struck Cornwell as *"a large man dressed in a suit, with a Beatles haircut"* who was *"a bit more mature"* than he had expected.

It is difficult to overstate the importance of Jet Black's role in the nascent Stranglers. Indeed, The Stranglers were his band in much the same way that Johnny Sox had been Hans Wärmling's. On the one hand, Black was an extremely adept and practical man who, on a limited budget, provided all the necessities for the band to maintain its precarious early existence, and, on the other, his dark philosophical view of the world as being in the sway of hidden, manipulative forces came to be the framework within which the group's creative output evolved. Indeed, there is a curious resonance in the way that The Stranglers, as "the men in black", were in thrall to Black's sinister worldview and dependent on his organisational abilities, and their greater fixation with The Meninblack, the putative alien force that engineered global events. There is a hint here, but no more than a hint, that the byzantine power structure within the band, which had the drummer as its locus, was being projected onto wider society.

The first major repercussion of Black's acceptance into the band was a move out of London to the commuter town of Guildford, where Black ran an off-licence, "The Jackpot", and an ice-cream business. Although it was a rather seedy location, The Jackpot was based in a three-storey building with bedrooms to house all the band members, rehearsal rooms, and parking space for the ice-cream van that was to double as the group's tour van. This move was significant in that it took the band out of the capital, and so existentially removed them from the beating heart of the music industry, and yet also encouraged them to be as self-sufficient as they possibly could be in this more arid creative environment. As a consequence, the group became outsiders, yet ones with considerable internal drive and determination. The first casualties of the new regime were the two remaining "foreigners", singer Gyrth Godwin and bassist Jan Knutsson, who left after the former was criticised by Black for his lack of productivity. According to Cornwell, the drummer *"wasn't that upset"* at their departure. It was probably at this moment, with the breaking of the remaining core of Johnny Sox, that the old band ended, and the project that became The Stranglers began. Local lad John Burnel was quickly recruited and provided with Knutsson's bass, and then a new, more intensive phase of writing and rehearsing commenced, which was augmented by Black locating a rehearsal space at a local village hall that allowed the embryonic new group to play at high volume.

It is clear that it was the formidable energy and resolve of Jet Black that steered the group through these wilderness years, when they were reputedly turned down by no less than 24 record companies. Financially supporting The Guildford Stranglers, as they now called themselves, was to cost him both his businesses and his marriage, and yet he was part of a creative unit that would miraculously allow him to express his own artistic vision. The group became a four-piece again when Cornwell persuaded Hans Wärmling to come over from Sweden and join this new group that had been born from the ashes of Johnny Sox. The contribution that the multi-instrumentalist made to the formation of The Stranglers during the winter of 1974-75 was by all accounts profound, but its recorded legacy is slight – the only officially released material being his composition of the music for "Strange Little Girl". Wärmling would increasingly chafe at the middle-of-the-road covers that the band incorporated into their set to secure concert bookings, his departure being eventually provoked by a request to learn the multitudinous chord changes of "Tie A Yellow Ribbon". And so, when Dave Greenfield, or rather his aunt, answered the Melody Maker advertisement for a keyboard player to replace the departed Swede, the foundations of The Stranglers were complete.

Because of the convoluted manner in which the band developed, and the idiosyncratic and uncompromising character of each of its individual members, the structure of The Stranglers was as far from the hierarchical ideal as possible. Power within the group flowed through hidden, labyrinthine channels that were invisible to outsiders, and this is one of the reasons that the group's litany of managers and promoters found them almost impossible to work with. The band's behaviour could be remarkably perverse, casually squandering opportunities that lesser groups would have envied. However, this behaviour had an internal logic; antagonising the outside world provided external enemies that allowed The Stranglers to project their conflicts outwards, thus attenuating any tensions that may have surfaced within the group. And just how significant these tensions may otherwise have been can be gauged by the havoc they left in their wake.

The egalitarian but fluid structure of The Stranglers was openly manifested in many ways. For example, despite the fact that the overwhelming majority of the songwriting was under-taken by Cornwell and Burnel, the songs themselves were credited to the group as a whole, so as to ensure that all the members benefited equally from any royalties that accrued. Early television performances are also revealing in that both Jet Black and Dave Greenfield stand while playing their instruments, indicating that they are not merely submissive workmen. In many of the performances, Black can be seen to wander away from his drum kit, sometimes joining Cornwell and Burnel at the microphone, again emphasising that he is a major figure within the group. During British television appearances, Cornwell and Burnel would often swap instruments, or even pretend to perform each other's vocals, again underlining the uncertain centre of gravity within the band. These gambits are generally interpreted as subversive interruptions of the conventions of mimed recorded playback, and together with Cornwell's occasional habit of singing far away from the microphone, or playing no-handed guitar solos, to some extent they were. But they were also the result of the unconscious compulsion of The Stranglers to reify their uncertain structure on the stage. Away from the comparative discipline of British television, the group's performances on continental television shows were even more anarchic, often starting with the entire band "playing" each other's instruments, and ending with the complete destruction of the studio set.

The picture cover for the band's debut album, *Rattus Norvegicus*, also undermines the conventional group hierarchy, with keyboard player Greenfield pictured at the front of the diorama, and singer Cornwell almost indistinguishable at the back. The cover for the third album, *Black And White*, would give the ominous figure of Jet Black prominence, with Cornwell and Burnel both adopting abject postures at the rear. Even the underlying structure of The Stranglers' music was treacherously abnormal, being rife with unusual time signatures and the occasional bar with a missing or added beat, a legacy of the jazz drumming of Chicago Mike. The comparatively low-status bass dominated the guitar, which had to compete for second billing with Dave Greenfield's snazzy keyboards. It was this mutable group structure that helped to give the band their intimidating hydra-headed aura, in which it was difficult to judge which of its constituent members was really the most dangerous. It was also a structure that could barely contain Cornwell's lippy antinomianism and Burnel's hair-trigger temper, but that was necessitated by the fact that each group member had at least some claim to authority. Cornwell and Burnel were the frontmen and chief songwriters, Greenfield was the most consummate musician, and Black was the most resourceful and experienced in the ways of business. The two major products of this structure, or rather contained anti-structure, would therefore be an intensively creative musical environment in which each member would be able to flourish in a way that would not have been possible in a "normal" band, and an insidiously paranoid worldview that would eventually spiral out of control.

This paranoia gained a framework with the concept of The Men In Black, which was simultaneously a conspiracy theory and a creation myth, which is to say a theology, and this in itself is appropriate. The philosopher of science Karl Popper noted that conspiracy theories were themselves a kind of theology; that they came *"from abandoning God and then asking 'who is in his place?'"* Thus conspiracy theories are in one sense the "rational" theologies of secular, atheistic societies. And, as the French theologian Jacques Ellul was to explain in *The Meaning Of The City*, if Man wants to abandon God, then firstly he must build a city.

The city cannot be reformed. Neither can she become other than what men have made of her. Nor can she escape from God's condemnation. Thus in spite of all the efforts of men of good will, in spite of those who have tried to make the cities more human, they are still formed of iron, steel, glass, and cement. The garden city, the show city. The brilliant city. They are all cities of death, made of dead things, condemned to death, and nothing can alter this fact. The mark of her builders and the judgements of God weigh her ruthlessly down. And everything she hoped in is condemned, her walls have crumbled to dust, her money is scattered, her power is annihilated. She has become the house of the demons who haunt the desert. 'The jackals will howl in her palaces, and the wild dogs in her mansions.'

In *The Meaning Of The City*, Ellul posited that the Bible, regardless of its many authors and diverse origins, adopts a consistent attitude toward the city, and that this attitude, no matter whether there is any historical evidence to verify the events that justify it, represents a psychological truth. He notes that the very first city, Enoch, was built by Cain, the first murderer, when he was banished east of Eden, to wander in the land of Nod. Cain, cursed by God, and mistakenly believing himself to no longer be under God's protection, reduces Him to an abstraction, and builds a city, which represents a new beginning, the beginning of civilisation. God's creation and the Garden of Eden become mere myths. In his city, Cain sets about remedying those needs which were formerly met by God's beneficence: he invents tools and crafts-manship to manipulate nature to his own ends, which are Man's ends. But the city, being the site where Man enacts his rebellion against God, and where the first murderer becomes the first builder, becomes a spiritual power in herself – one that is opposed to God and yet, far from being the summation of the efforts of the men who build her, is capriciously indifferent to their interests. Thinking they are working to improve their own interests, they are in fact working for her glory, and hers alone.

From this point, all the builders are in the mould of Cain, and all carry his curse. Nimrod, builder of Babylon and Nineveh, is a conqueror, and so the association of cities with warfare is estab-lished. Each of Nimrod's cities represents a conquest, embodied in their name. For example, the great city of Resen is named after the bridle of a horse, Man's first tool for harnessing and controlling natural power. In Babylon, the mythical Babel, a great tower, is built to the heavens so that its inhabitants can, for the first time, look down and name themselves. However, it is only Yahweh who has the power to give names, and so he visits them and confounds their speech. Although the story of the Tower of Babel is usually thought of as a myth to explain the existence of different languages, for Ellul it is an allegory for the inability of intellectualised urban men to understand one another, even if they speak the same words in the same language; the pursuit of power, a characteristic of the city, creates allegiances and ideologies that corrupt mutual understanding. From another viewpoint, we can also recognise the Babel story as an allegory of the tendency of the supernatural to confound rational attempts at creating structure – it is a myth that seeks to acknowledge the principle of anti-structure.

Ellul then moves to Egypt, the land of sorrow, where the Pharaoh has enslaved Israel, and has forced the chosen people to build his granary cities of Raamses and Pithom, and notes that this is where the Bible establishes the relationship both between the city and slavery, and between the city and economics. Worse, because Pithom is a shrine to the false religion of Thom, the sun god, the city also reveals itself to be the place where false idols proliferate. The quest for wealth and privilege within the city's walls creates a lust for objects in which the cheapest goods on sale become men's souls; and so, in the words of John of Patmos, the city becomes *"the mother of harlots"*. For Ellul, Babylon is the prototypical city. All the cities have their own individual characters, but they are at one and the same time all Babylon, nest of warfare, slavery, prostitution and false idols.

And they are all cursed. God will tolerate their crimes and idolatries, their persecutions of the church of Israel only for so long. Every city lies in the shadow of the exterminating angel, who will destroy them by sword, or by plague, or by fire, so that *"no stone will be left standing upon another"*. Babylon, Nineveh,

Sodom, Gomorrah, Jericho, all the cities that defied God were visited by his wrath, and there was no sifting of the righteous from the non-righteous. The punishment was collective because it is the city itself that is set in opposition to the Lord, and it is the spiritual power of the city that defines the consciousness of its people, and not the other way around. And so it will be with the modern city of today. *"The jackals will howl in her palaces, and the wild dogs in her mansions."*

It is this sense of the city being dirty, sacrilegious and doomed that pervades The Stranglers' debut album *Rattus Norvegicus*, released in April 1977. The success of the band in securing a recording contract with RCA had been the result of two years of hard work, with its extensive writing, rehearsing and touring. The group had shown enough promise to be signed up by the Albion Agency, a management company run by Dai Davies and Derek Savage, who, via their booker Ian Grant, had the clout to secure residences for the band at influential venues such as the Nashville, the Red Cow, and the Hope & Anchor. As the band became drawn into the maelstrom of the embryonic punk scene, so they had re-located to London, and the LP wasn't so much an evocation of that dying imperial city, as a reification of it in sound.

Rattus Norvegicus is, primarily, a condemnation of the city. For The Stranglers, London is essentially a sewer, one that exists in an eternal night, its denizens (not least the group themselves) no more than vermin. It is one of the most perverse and repellent musical visions ever conceived, and one that would provoke bitter controversy. Even today, listening to *Rattus* makes one feel in need of a wash afterwards. Most of the antagonism that was directed toward the record was provoked by the rich seam of misogyny that permeated it like effluent. And yet, the righteous ire that the band's sexism, both real and perceived, inspired is itself a curious anomaly, misogyny hardly being a novelty within the history of popular music, or even that of the punk movement, despite its pretensions to a "progressive" political stance.

In an infamous review, the NME's Phil McNeill disdainfully clasped the LP with rhetorical tongs and condemned its *"permanent immaturity"* and *"godawful, vindictive reality"*. However, he came closest to stumbling on a real insight when he said *"don't tell me it's just The Rolling Stones and 'Brown Sugar' however many years on, because that was pretty pathetic too."* There was, in fact, something different about The Stranglers' misogyny. After all, the sexism of the Rolling Stones' "Under My Thumb" or Led Zeppelin's "Whole Lotta Love" was triumphant, overpowering – the conquering of all resistance. The misogyny that The Stranglers evoked was entirely the opposite – frustrated, impotent, and glowering with suppressed rage. *Rattus Norvegicus* may have been unprecedentedly brutal in its depiction of violence against women, but what few critics noticed at the time was just how melancholy it was. It is one of the saddest records ever made, and it is this conflation of rage and regret that gives it its chilling emotional authenticity.

This is because The Stranglers' misogyny is reflexive – it is misogyny that exposes the mechanisms of misogyny, and this is in turn what made it so scandalous to male critics. This reflexivity is most apparent on the opening track, "Sometimes". The song is, at the most basic level, a re-write of The Doors' "Love Her Madly", but also an inversion of the sentiment expressed in the original. If "Love Her Madly" is a belated admission of emotional and psychological dependency, then "Sometimes" is a vain denial of it. As with The Doors, the very sound of The Stranglers locates us in an urban, nocturnal setting. As Burnel's predatory bass paces around the block, the multi-tracked guitars and keyboards trace exquisite flecks of light, like headlights shimmering on a rain-washed street. It's a reflective sound, one that recalls those eerie moments when experience is being committed to memory while it is in the process of unfolding, and then the opening line hits the listener like a cosh:

Some day I'm gonna smack your face

The immediacy of Cornwell's vocals pulls us out of our reverie, as he doles out his prescription for retributory violence:

Somebody's gonna to call your bluff
Somebody's gonna to treat you rough

But then a strange thing happens. As his threats escalate and become more and more explicit, we begin to realise that he's on his own, that the song is a monologue and not a dialogue; that Cornwell is in his own violent reverie. He is assaulting his own memories, perhaps in order to model the real violence to come, but perhaps also because imagined violence is the only option available.

You're way past your station
Beat you,
Honey
Till you drop

Cornwell based the lyrics on an incident that ended a relationship he'd been having with a local girl while he was living above The Jackpot in Guildford. As he related to Jim Drury in *Song By Song*:

After a year or so together I suspected she was seeing someone else and went round to see her house at about ten o'clock one morning, but she wasn't there and hadn't been back all night. When she turned up I could smell sex on her and I slapped her. I didn't beat her up because I don't think violence is a solution to anything, but I did get angry and slapped her. I was using violence as a release of emotion and the lyrics to 'Sometimes' came out of that.

I'd never done it before and I've never done it since. It's a very odd situation, not only just to find out that someone's cheating on you, but to actually catch them coming back with the smell on them. It's a horrific situation to be in and I'll never forget it.

But "Sometimes" isn't a song about hitting a woman; it's a song about the compulsive need for the catharsis of hitting a woman. It yearns for the release of tension and emotion that striking a blow would yield, and yet implicitly recognises the long trail of guilt and regret that would inevitably follow. Cornwell's threats are impotent, and they would remain so even if they were carried out, because to strike out merely underlines the level of emotional dependence. In this way, the feelings the song evokes are liminal; the cascading guitar solo, much inspired by Robby Krieger, sounds like nothing so much as a long sigh, an acknowledgment of futility. And the key to understanding The Stranglers' misogyny is embodied within this ambivalence – what they, and perhaps all men, despise is not women, but their own desire for them; the great chain of dependency that underlies all the other chains with which the city ties them down.

And so Cornwell is alone, trapped in an interstitial realm bounded by fury and despair, seeking solace in fantasies of violence that may never happen, and would serve little purpose if they did. And this experience is common enough, and not exclusively to men either. It is the currency of vulnerability and dependency, and can never be assuaged by right-thinking, or ideological consistency, or reforming legislation. It is this unpleasant truth that the band's critics found so unacceptable.

If "Sometimes" is a personalised evocation of the agonised predicaments that bind and direct human relations, then the next song on the album, "Goodbye Toulouse" is the first manifestation of the group's intention to give them a cosmological explanation. Indeed, if The Stranglers had a project (and both Cornwell and Burnel would refer to the band as being "a cause") then it was to find a rational explanation for the misery and corruption of Earthly existence. Such concerns are normally the province of religion, and so it was inevitable that the group, following all other rationalist attempts to discern meaning and order in the cosmos, would end up pursuing what would turn out to be theology dressed up in the raiments of modern science. When secular humanism attempts the reflexive task of examining its own foundations, it turns mystical, and, lacking the religious understanding of the dangers of the liminal realm of the supernatural, it can rapidly descend into paranoia and madness. As Cornwell was to explain:

We were getting into Nostradamus at the time, and one of his predictions was that Toulouse in France would suffer a cataclysmic event and be destroyed. It just so happens that there's a nuclear power station in Toulouse so John (Burnel) and I thought this event could be an atomic mishap. So it was a song of goodbye to the town, and the explosion at the end is supposed to represent an atomic meltdown at Toulouse.

In fact, the sixteenth-century prophet referred to cataclysmic events in Toulouse in a number of his quatrains, or four-lined verses, and as with all his prophecies, their interpretation is subject to a great deal of contention, and this is no surprise as we can see that the fundamental premise of the Nostradamus phenomenon negates one of the causal assumptions implicit in Western science – that time can only move in one direction, and so future events are not directly accessible to those in the past or present. To believe in the efficacy of Nostradamus is to accept the possibility of precognition, and thus the reality of paranormal phenomena. It is fitting that it is the interpretation of Nostradamus's texts that is so controversial, as this lies in the field of hermeneutics, named after Hermes, the trickster god. It is also appropriate that false or deliberately exaggerated versions of his prophecies have been used in hoaxes, as this too indicates the presence of the Trickster constellation.

The popularity of the prophecies of Nostradamus have a perennial allure, but they were particularly enhanced by the post-war occult publishing boom, which brought forth many and various interpretations of his work, and it wasn't until the mid-1980s that French scholars began the belated rationalising task of subjecting them to critical analysis, and rejecting many of the most lurid and fanciful readings. Before this, the prophecies were subjected to an almost dialectical process in which these catastrophic visions of the future were creatively misinterpreted to resonate with events in the past, such the rise of Napoleon and Hitler, thus granting them a purported greater stochastic probability of predicting the future. In this sense they were an example of George Hansen's assertion, contra Weber, that magic is not expunged from disenchanted Western society, but is banished to the margins ready to infect the rational superstructure at any available opportunity.

Nostradamus's quatrains, with their unusual syntax, word play, and language switches, combined with the inevitable errors implicit in modern interpretation and translation, are sufficiently ambiguous as to facilitate any meaning that the interpreter wishes to infer. Nevertheless, their tone of impending catastrophe would have a peculiar resonance in Cold War metropolises living under the four-minute warning of nuclear destruction. In this sense, "Goodbye Toulouse" is not only an evocation of the exterminating angel that hovered over every city of the era, it is the first example of The Stranglers' attempt to utilise the irrationalism of the occult as a tool to explain the experience of rationalised modern society. The lyrics, written by Burnel, also evoked the tristesse of urban life:

I walked your streets in fear
I washed your streets with tears
Toulouse

Paula, a medieval courtesan, leans out from her high balcony to view the scene below, hinting once again that the city, even this doomed, melancholy one, is the nest of harlots. However, it would be the following song that would make the connection explicit.

"London Lady" is at first glance simply a patronising put-down of a groupie, the first verse locating it in the specificity of the capital's music scene:

Little lady with Dingwall's bullshit
You're so stupid foetid brainwaves
Little lady what really happens
When you see mirrors you get the shivers

These sentiments were roundly condemned by the band's critics, who argued that the title of the song gave it a generality in its criticism of female promiscuity. As such, it was simply a re-statement of the familiar patriarchal position that promiscuity is acceptable for men, but unacceptable for women. Burnel's attempted justification of his lyrics only strengthened the case for the prosecution:

We were drawing lots on who was going to screw this female column writer, and someone said, 'But it'd be like chucking a sausage up the Mersey Tunnel.' Someone else said 'dangling a piece of string in a bucket'. It's been done before, so we decided it wasn't valid to do it. It's just about some chicks in a very small scene.

At the time, the target of the song was believed to be the NME columnist Caroline Coon, something that was subsequently denied by the band, who insisted that the subject of the song was a composite of a number of different women. Coon herself would later respond trenchantly:

> *In 1977 the New Musical Express stated that the Stranglers' song*
> *'London Lady' was written about Caroline Coon. In fact, the song*
> *is a woman-hating fantasy with lyrics indicative of what clinicians*
> *call 'small penis anxiety' and evidence of the sexism and misogyny*
> *that contaminates the male dominated music industry to this day.*

Which, like so many criticisms of The Stranglers, passes tantalisingly close to genuine perceptiveness before somewhat missing the mark. The anxiety of which Coon speaks is revealed in the second verse of the song, which would conjure the grotesque, comic surrealism of René Magritte:

> *Making love to the Mersey Tunnel*
> *With a sausage. Have you ever been to Liverpool?*
> *Please don't talk much it burns my ears*
> *Tonight you've talked for a thousand years*

The metaphor of a small limp sausage confronting a giant tunnel-vagina obviously works in two distinctive ways; as a symbol both of the vast pollution of female promiscuity, and of male impotence in the face of it. Once again, The Stranglers are emphasizing male weakness rather than strength. But, at another level, what is being suggested is the idea of the city as the ultimate woman – the city as the pre-eminent whore. The microcosm of the Dingwall's groupie is reflected in the macrocosm of the vampiric nature of London (or indeed Liverpool) itself. And this is the queasy sensation that underlays all of *Rattus Norvegicus*; that the thousand year-old city is a living, organic being, replete with pulsing, throbbing, tunnel-wombs and sewer-colons beneath the gleaming, phallic towers that are the normal sources of pride and wonder.

It is also striking that Caroline Coon should have been proposed as the inspiration for such a metaphor, as much of her early work as an artist, including paintings such as "My Beautiful

Cunt" and "Cuntucopia" were a *"political response to pathological hatred and fear of female genitalia"*. Her feminist writings rail against the classification of women as "whores", which she sees as a regrettable side effect of the greater freedom entailed by Women's Liberation. Her proposed solution, to legalise prostitution and make it a respectable profession, is a paragon example of an anti-structural attempt to reverse a social binary.

The Stranglers' putative sexism became the lightning rod through which the general disquiet that the band generated was channeled, and was an issue that they were invariably interrogated on during the interviews they gave to the music press. It is clear that most journalists were looking for them to at best repudiate, and at the very least clarify, the misogynistic content of their lyrics. Naturally, this is the one thing the band refused to do, and this frequently resulted in interviews becoming dangerously tense and hostile. It should be pointed out here that The Stranglers' lyrics were, in their treatment of the violence and aggression directed at women, far from being the most extreme of their genre. Both The Birthday Party and Throbbing Gristle recorded songs that expressed cathartic release in sexual violence, but, unlike The Stranglers, they foregrounded their position as social documenters and "artists", and emphasised the purely representational nature of their work. In essence, it was The Stranglers' refusal to make such an open declaration – that their misogyny was simply an act – that formed the kernel of the suspicion that was to envelop them.

The band's general response to charges of sexism was to refuse to acknowledge the accusation, to present a front of confused ingenuousness. This would occasionally be leavened with a sardonic witticism from Cornwell, for example when he declared that the reason he put women on a pedestal was so that he could look up their skirts. This strategy tended to frustrate interrogators, as it added another layer of ambivalence upon an existing one. After all, it was known that both Cornwell and

Burnel were university-educated, and were therefore presumed too intelligent for this kind of base sexism, and yet here they were, pretending not to understand what sexism actually was, while casually providing examples of it! It was the underlying suspicion among the music press that they might, just might, be being mocked, and that the band's misogyny really was just pure provocation, that no doubt reinforced the hostility that they felt towards The Stranglers. And this is not difficult to understand, because even today it is difficult to really ascertain just how much the group "meant it".

In a typically circumlocutory interview with the NME's Lynn Hanna, Hugh Cornwell was asked, regarding the band's early songs, whether he was playing on women's insecurities. *"Not at all. I was playing on my guitar"* came the reply, and the conversation predictably deteriorated from that point onwards. But the friction generated by the band's refusal to define, let alone repudiate, their attitude did serve a particular purpose – it cemented their position as outsiders, and provided them with plenty of external enemies. This, in turn, attenuated any internal conflicts they might otherwise have had, and reinforced their perception of the world as being fundamentally hostile and manipulated by dark, unseen forces.

The very first glimpses of what these forces might be were revealed on two songs written by Burnel about his then girlfriend, Choosey Susie. The eponymous song "Choosey Susie", which was included as a free single with *Rattus Norvegicus*, included the tantalising line *"there's a lot of stars up there, but there's a lot more we can't see"*, before making a telling Biblical reference to Lot's wife, who looked back at the razing of Sodom. In "Princess Of The Streets", Susie is langorously referred to as *"a piece of meat"*, in what would be the first airing of the perennial Stranglers theme of cannibalism. Yet again, we see a woman being identified with the city, both alluring and treacherous.

However, it is with "Hanging Around", which crowned the

first side of the LP, that the band's evocation of the spiritual decay inherent in the city finds its most consummate expression, as we are given a guided tour of the milieu around the band's stamping ground of Earls Court. Starting *"down the Court Road early with the hustlers big and burly"* we eventually find ourselves in The Coleherne, a gay leather bar on the Old Brompton Road; a venue that Burnel visited with Choosey Susie, and found suitably intimidating and impressive, and which would later provide the venue for a trio of serial killers to pick up their victims. The song presents a vision of sex as spiritually empty, as purely concerned with economic transaction or pharmacological compulsion, in either case a draining, vampiric experience. In the city the cheapest thing for sale is the souls of men. And not just the souls of any men, but the souls of the greatest of men too, because

> *Christ has told his mother, Christ he's told her not to bother*
> *Because he's alright in the city, he's high above the ground*
> *He's just hanging around*

And so we see the rent boys of Earls Court elevated, each one of them, to the status of Messiah, with London as their own Golgotha, and Jesus simultaneously lowered to the status of rent boy. It is an infernal vision in which prostitution, and the compulsions that it feeds on, are revealed to be the very lifeblood of the city, turning its vendors and clients into husks. And yet, what is the strange power that creates and shapes all this misery? Where The Stranglers diverge from Ellul is that they do not identify it as the city itself, wicked though that might be. After all, the city is only the place where men abandon God, and allow His Son to sell himself in the street. No, The Stranglers feel there is another power that stands behind the city, and yet is currently obscure, indistinct.

It is on the second song of side two of the album, "(Get A) Grip (On Yourself)", that we first get a real insight into the underlying structure of the band's *weltanschauung*. "Grip" is a deeply strange song mainly because of the precognitive elements in Cornwell's lyrics – it looks to the criminal past from which the band emerged (*"begged, borrowed, sometimes I admit I even stole"*) and intimates that prison is Cornwell's inevitable destination (*"suffering convictions on a two-way stretch inside"*). In a world as corrupt as Earth, the righteous are made criminals, and the worst crime they can commit is to document this corruption in music, by *"playing rock'n'roll"*. And The Stranglers did perform on behalf of criminals, playing benefit gigs for PROP, the organisation for the Preservation of the Rights of Prisoners, and even playing to the inmates of Chelmsford Prison. The song is also a comment on the punishing nature of the music industry, with its treadmill of schedules that, in the band's early career, seemed to offer no reward.

However, the oddest, and most significant, moment in "Grip" is when Cornwell beckons extra-terrestrial life to descend from the heavens, and join the band:

Stranger from another planet, welcome to our hole
Just strap on a guitar and we'll play some rock and roll

This is the very first invite to the aliens who would eventually gain form as the Meninblack, and it is invariably overlooked. And yet, this invocation would have a number of uncanny resonances. Firstly, "Grip" would be the group's first single, and it would also be the first instance when their career would be impeded by mysterious external sabotage. Released on 28th January 1977, it entered the singles chart at Number 44, and was expected to enter the Top 20 the following week, but, due to an error by chart compilers BMRB, instead found itself outside the Top 50, its rightful place being occupied by the German disco group Silver Convention. Hugh Cornwell would later air his conviction that this "error" was no accident, yet it is also possible to see this incident as an early sign that what George Hansen calls "the Trickster constellation" was beginning to form. As we shall see, just as The Stranglers would become increasingly indistinguishable from their extra-terrestrial alter-egos, so it would also become more and more difficult to differentiate between the actions, both overt and covert, of their enemies, and the band's own Herculean efforts at self-sabotage. Stranger still was the detail revealed in the photo of the group on the inner sleeve of the album, where in the background can be seen a mysterious figure in the classic apparel, of trilby and trenchcoat, of the Men In Black – another indication that The Stranglers were on the cusp of The Goblin Universe. Curiously, four years later, in a radio interview with Tim Sommers of WNYU, Burnel would anachronistically claim that the figure was indeed a Man In Black, and had been placed there deliberately.

"Grip" was preceded on *Rattus Norvegicus* by what would become the band's second single, and first big hit, "Peaches", which would reach Number 8 in the charts in May 1977. "Peaches" would see the band taking a temporary break from the city in order to soak up the sun and top up the wank bank. Narrated by Cornwell in his best sar-car-stic stage patter, the lyrics were a pervy-satirical tour-de-force, at once reveling in the exposure of female flesh while revealing the self-deceptions and circumlocutions inherent in the voyeuristic mind. After all, with the line *"strolling along, minding my own business"*, the song even starts with a lie, and it is clear that the increasingly heated internal monologue has no chance of being acted out in reality. It's not long, however, before the evening sets in, and Cornwell's mind is returning to the street and the sewer, and, after the psychotic masculine protest of Burnel's "Ugly", that's exactly where we end up.

"Down In The Sewer" is the crescendo of *Rattus Norvegicus*, and, as Cornwell was to tell Jim Drury, was an allegory of London, as the band viewed it from their base in rural

Chiddingford, where the piece was first composed in 1975. The track consists of four movements; starting with the instrumental "Falling", there follows the vocal "Down In the Sewer", then the further instrumentals "Trying To Get Out Again" and "Rats Rally", the titles suggesting that once the sewer of city life is entered, there is little chance of escape:

People say you shouldn't stay down here too long
Lose your sense of light and dark
Lose your sense of smell

The sewer represents the repressed elements of the city, being the repository of human wastes, the discharges of gluttony and sexual desire, where mankind's distant biological cousins the rats make their home. Like humans, rats are adaptable, voracious and ubiquitous; they adapt to man's constructions whether on land or on the oceans, as though they were his own shadow. Indeed with their social hierarchies, based on fiercely contested dominance and submission, there is an eerie consonance between rat societies and human ones. More than a mere metaphor, The Stranglers see the rat world and the human world as interchangeable, different representations of the same pattern. And this pattern must come from somewhere else.

There was also one more intriguing synchronicity connected with this final song on the album. *Rattus Norvegicus* was recorded at the partly subterranean TW studios on Fulham Palace Road, and, as producer Martin Rushent was to relate to Chris Wade:

The control room was under a launderette. So it was the last night of the sessions and the last thing we did was "Down In The Sewer" for "Rattus". It must have been no more than half an hour after we left, that the rear wall of the studio collapsed and Fulham Palace sewer emptied its contents into the studio. Which, I think, is really odd.

Rattus Norvegicus was a great commercial success, peaking at No.4 and remaining in the album charts for 34 weeks. The recording sessions for *Rattus* had also been so productive that enough material had been recorded to comprise half of the next LP. In fact, Rushent would later describe The Stranglers as *"the tightest band I ever took into the studio."* The choice of the dingy TW studios, with its sparse furnishings and cheap mixing consoles, as the venue for the recording of the first three albums was a somewhat perverse one, and was made purely on a whim, as Rushent was to relate to The Burning Up Times:

> *During this period, I heard a tape of a band who recorded at TW and it sounded good. It was a bit rough but the sound was good. The band was called Trickster, a standard rock band of the time, but there was just something about the sound I thought was really good.*

The Stranglers, Martin Rushent, and the gritty sound of TW Studios, had proved a powerful and efficient combination, and Rushent was to subsequently claim that Burnel in particular riled at the possibility of him working with other bands. According to Rushent, Burnel informed him (erroneously) that The Doors' producer Paul Rothschild had only worked with that particular group, to which Rushent replied that the only way he could exclusively work with The Stranglers was if they made him their fifth, studio-bound, member, with a concomitant share of earnings. It was the band's equivocal response, along with the increasingly experimental nature of their music, that ensured the two parties went their separate ways the following year.

The group's second album, *No More Heroes* was released on 23rd September 1977, a mere five months after the debut. The album arrived on the back of two further Top Ten singles, "Something Better Change" and the title track. "Something Better Change" had been released in July as a double A-side with the similarly rabble-rousing "Straighten Out", Cornwell's lyrics opening with the sinister pronouncement:

...and the First Commandment reads that human flesh and blood is sacred...until there is no more food.

This line was partly inspired by Robert Heinlein's "Stranger In A Strange Land", a satirical science-fiction novel in which a Martian with superhuman psychic abilities visits a consumerist America, founds a populist church, and teaches his disciples powerful psychokinetic abilities in order to create a new kind of human called Homo Superior, which will inevitably come to dominate and replace those who refuse to follow them. It was also a reference to the sense of British society starting to fall apart. As Cornwell was to tell Jim Drury:

We'd recently had the three-day week and there were so many jobless, it was a serious state of affairs. There were times when you'd taken so many drugs that you thought things would start breaking down ... it's a suggestion that if anarchy did take place and the government broke down, it might get to the stage where there wouldn't be any food and people would start eating each other.

This alarming scenario would be revisited by Cornwell on the B-side of the single that followed "No More Heroes". On "Rok It To The Moon", the flip-side of "Five Minutes", he escapes from a doomed near-future Earth on a one-way trip to its nearest satellite:

I'm looking forward to the year of '88
Eating each other I fear before that date

...where he voyeuristically watches the chaos that he has left behind:

Play creator face new situations
Watch the humans create new frustrations

What is intriguing in this scenario is that Cornwell himself becomes an extra-terrestrial, and this gives him the opportunity to manipulate the previously indigenously chaotic conditions on Earth. This provides an insight into the inherently reflexive quality that was to pervade The Stranglers' conception of The Meninblack. The world is an inherently dismal place whose inhabitants can barely restrain themselves from tearing each other apart, and yet it is also the case that these appalling conditions arise from outside manipulation. Simultaneously, the group are particularly the victims of these dark manipulators, and yet they also strongly identify with the power that these putative beings are able to wield. It is no accident that The Stranglers began to refer to themselves as The Men In Black at exactly the same time as they evolved their notions of the alien Meninblack.

The eponymous "No More Heroes" became one of the band's best-known songs, and is generally viewed as a lament for the absence of inspiring figures in rationalised modern life. However, the "heroes" that Cornwell name-checks in the song are a distinctly unusual bunch, who at first sight don't seem to belong to any coherent category. What is it that unites Don Quixote's literary sidekick Sancho Panza, the Hungarian art forger Elmyr de Hory, the provocative comedian Lenny Bruce, and the revolutionary Leon Trotsky? None of these men, it must be said, are normally considered to encompass the classic virtues. The answer, of course, is that all of them were in some sense anti-structural, in that they are either associated with deception or disruption.

Elmyr de Hory operated a profitable business in flooding the art world with thousands of forgeries of the work of prestigious artists such as Picasso, Matisse and Renoir. Being both Jewish and homosexual, de Hory was inevitably on the margins of society, and had experienced imprisonment in a German concentration camp. His post-war career as a forger was profoundly anti-structural, as not only was it based on deception, but it also had the effect of de-legitimising the international art market and the "experts" who gained prestige and status by policing it. His fakes were so plausible that they even called into question the concept of "authenticity" itself. He was unmasked as a forger, and, after being imprisoned in Spain for his homosexuality, he committed suicide in 1976, on learning of his impending extradition to France on fraud charges.

Lenny Bruce, also Jewish, was so anti-structural as to almost beggar belief. Born Leonard Schneider in Brooklyn, New York, he was discharged from the US Navy in 1945 after managing to convince his ship's medical officer that he was experiencing homosexual urges. His early showbusiness career saw him performing as the master of ceremonies at strip clubs, and an early brush with the law occurred when he impersonated a priest to solicit donations for the "Brother Mathias Foundation", a fictional leper colony in British Guyana. The real purpose of the "Foundation" was for Bruce to earn enough money to enable his wife to give up stripping.

As Bruce's stage performances grew more popular, they concurrently became more transgressive, breaching taboos on politics, patriotism, race and sex. A hero of the counter-culture, he attempted to blend the spontaneity of jazz into his comic persona, while, mimicking his jazz heroes, his personal life devolved into a miasma of drugs and sexual promiscuity. He inevitably aroused the suspicion of the authorities, and was arrested on numerous occasions for obscenity. He was barred from performing in Britain in 1962 as an "undesirable alien", and in November 1964, after a highly publicised six-month trial, was finally found guilty of obscenity by a Manhattan court. He was sentenced to four months in a workhouse, although he was still on bail awaiting a decision on his appeal when he died of a heroin overdose in August 1966, having been blacklisted by almost every nightclub in America.

Leon Trotsky, who may well have been the greatest trickster of the twentieth century, was born Lev Bronstein (Jewish again) in what is now Ukraine, but which was at the time of his birth part of the Russian Empire. A competent revolutionary from his early twenties, he played a key role in the October Revolution of 1917, and was especially effective as the head of the Red Army during the Civil War that lasted through to 1920. After Lenin's death in 1924, however, his ability to influence the political course of the embryonic Soviet Union was undermined by the machine-bureaucrat Josef Stalin, and he was expelled from the USSR in 1929.

Effectively isolated in Mexico, Trotsky railed against the "Stalinist Bureaucracy" that had turned the Soviet Union into a continent-wide prison camp, and had refused to propagate the Revolution internationally due to its doctrine of Socialism In One Country. Trotsky's idea of "permanent revolution" was conceived as an expedient means of progressing the proletarian revolution in those countries that were too economically or polit-ically disadvantaged to first generate a bourgeois democratic one. The onus was thus on the proletariat to undertake the burdens of both revolutionary tasks concomitantly by forming a workers' state and appropriating capitalist plant and property. However, any permanent revolution in one country alone would be vulnerable to counter-attack from the capitalist states, so it therefore had to be an international programme. This was essen-tially a prescription for turning the hierarchical structures of the entire capitalist world system upside down, and was possibly the most anti-structural political ideology in history.

Small wonder then that Trotsky inspired not only fear and loathing in the liberal democratic states, but also among his erstwhile comrades in the Revolution. Trotsky became a kind of Marxist version of anti-matter, and, even after the period of de-

Stalinisation under the leadership of Khrushchev, his works remained prohibited in the Soviet Union. By this time he was long dead, murdered by the agents of the Stalinist Bureaucracy at his home in Mexico City in May 1940. Nevertheless, Trotskyism lives on today, and remains notoriously volatile and prone to antagonistic fissions, as well as suffering the perennial embarrassment of its most ambitious devotees deciding that, at least in practical terms, permanent revolution is much more easily achievable from the political Right.

Sancho Panza was in many ways the odd character out, as he represents the reality principle in Cervantes' novel. His master Don Quixote, the former Alonso Quixana, lives in an imaginary world of chivalry in which washbasins are knightly shields and windmills are giants, yet, as the cultural historian Morris Berman has pointed out, he was an anachronism even by the time the novel was published at the beginning of the seventeenth century – a man who was conducting his behaviour according to the sympathetic symbolism of an earlier era, prone to enchantments and paeans to a "golden age" where property and war didn't exist – just as the new "mechanical philosophy" was starting to take root in Western culture. If Sancho Panza is a hero, it is because although he is a realist, and in many ways a "modern" man, he has the grace not to break his master's illusions, representative of an age when reality was not so sharply defined.

Trotsky presented the same kind of ideal role model for Hugh Cornwell that Yukio Mishima did for JJ Burnel. The Russian revolutionary was analytical, competent, decisive, and left a vast swathe of destruction in his wake. While de Hory and Bruce engaged in deceptions and transgressed social boundaries, Trotsky's ideas erased international ones. He was a kind of ur-trickster, promising a world in which all hierarchy and status would be overthrown in an endless global communitas. However, Cornwell should have taken note of what did happen to these three "heroes" – the forces of bureaucratic authority destroyed them all.

The *No More Heroes* LP was more combative than the debut, and where the themes from *Rattus* were reprised they were exaggerated almost to the point of grotesquerie. "Peasant In The Big Shitty", inspired by an acid trip that JJ Burnel had experienced in a telephone booth in Guildford, was a darkly hilarious piece of schlock-horror played in queasy 9/4 time. Dave Greenfield's vocals channel Vincent Price as he presents a Roger Corman tableau of the Vampire City.

"Bring On The Nubiles" inflated the group's previous sexual innuendo to an almost absurd degree, the motivation, according to Cornwell, being *"now that we've got this muscle, let's see what we can get away with."* The sentiments behind the pornographic lyrics are truly appalling, irresistibly so, and the compulsive bass and orgasmatronic Mini Moog solo make the song a disgracefully guilty pleasure. In every sense, it's a great song for Catholics. It also provided a useful stick with which to prod the more Puritan elements of the music press, with Burnel informing the NME:

Hugh happens to have this thing towards under-age girls. He'll get arrested for it one day, but that's his quirk ... 'nubilicness', as espoused by The Stranglers, has developed into quite a philosophy, a kind of aesthetic.

Cornwell himself took a less fanciful view of the song, introducing it onstage by declaring *"I don't know what all this fuss is about child abuse. When I was a child, I used to abuse myself."*

Yet, underneath the dazzling malice of the *No More Heroes* album, another source of tension was becoming apparent, and that was the arduous work rate demanded by the record company. *Rattus Norvegicus* had been recorded in only six days, with the additional material required for *No More Heroes* taking an additional fourteen days. The band, under the watchful studio eye of Martin Rushent, would release their first three LPs in the space of just over a year, an astonishing level of productivity. However, United Artists continually demanded more from the band, and the strain was reflected in Dave Greenfield's pay-off at the end of "Dead Ringer":

Productivity … Credibility … Impossibility

The critical disdain also continued with the press reviews of the new album. The review that would prove to have the most far-reaching consequences was that written by Jon Savage in Sounds. Although it is often described as an entirely hostile write-up, it was in fact a deeply ambivalent and conflicted piece, and offered a fascinating insight into the ambiguous feelings that the band provoked. For a start, Savage openly acknowledged the technical excellence of The Stranglers, stating *"Half the album is full of very strong material, songs which are ridiculously catchy and well-constructed … the rhythm section is simply very tight, relentless, while the organ that fleshes the sound out … holds some kind of magical power with its hypnotic swell … oh yes, they can do it…"* However, he instinctively recoiled at the inscrutable antagonism that pervaded everything the group were associated with – *"what comes off the album, with its deliberate, unrelenting wallowing, is the chill of death."* Reading between the lines, it becomes apparent that Savage liked The Stranglers, but hated himself for doing so.

The Sounds review then repeated a common refrain of the era; the exasperation that obviously intelligent people, who could be marching forwards in the vanguard of social progress, were choosing instead to immerse themselves in the most primordial social atavism: *"No amount of 'intellectual' rationalisation can get round the fact that too many lyrix are dumb. Dumb – and Cornwell patently isn't … it sounds like everyone's intelligence is being insulted, yours, mine, and that of this record's creators…"*

Although Savage's review was impatient and irritable, it didn't close the door on the band. He just expected better things from them in the future. The hypersensitive JJ Burnel, on the other hand, took the review as a personal attack. As he would later tell Gary Kent:

> *I tracked him down one night to The Red Cow, and I punched his lights out right there in front of Jake Riviera, Andrew Lauder – our A&R guy – Elvis Costello, Nick Lowe, all these people saw what I did. So yeah, we made a lot of enemies, bless 'em, and these people got in a lot of influential positions within the music industry and literature … but we weren't gonna suck up to these cunts.*

What is notable about Burnel's attack on Savage, above and beyond the physical violence which would have been shocking enough in itself, is that the location of the assault, among a throng of influential scenesters, reveals that it was also an attack on the Sounds journalist's status. Savage was made of sterner stuff, however, and, over the ensuing decades, his increasingly influential position as the unofficial curator of the punk movement enabled him to give The Stranglers an object lesson in how to engineer status diminution.

Nonetheless, this incident initiated a series of aggressively humiliating pranks that were played on journalists. Record Mirror's Ronnie Gurr, once considered an ally of the band, was, after a negative review of *Euroman Cometh*, bundled on to Burnel's tour bus by the Finchley Boys, and driven to the location of the Euroband's next gig at Hemel Hempstead, where the intention was to strip him naked, tie him to a chair, and deposit him onstage for the encore. Gurr managed to escape down a stair well and find the local police station, leaving Burnel spending the rest of the evening hiding from the law. Also in 1979, the NME's Deanne Pearson, in one of the most ungentlemanly incidents in the history of popular music, was abandoned in the Portuguese countryside after The Stranglers had completed the video shoot for the "Nuclear Device" single. The most infamous incident involved the French writer Philippe Manoeuvre, as Burnel himself was to remember:

We were recording 'The Raven' in Paris to save tax. This young reporter kept hassling us, so I agreed if he came along, I would accord him an interview. So I took him to the first floor of the Eiffel Tower, 300 feet up, de-bagged him, and tied him with gaffer tape to one of the girders and left him there.

At least some of the responsibility for these pranks lay with the group's publicist Alan Edwards, who set up the kidnap of Ronnie Gurr, and who subscribed to the dictum that any publicity was good publicity. In the short term this may have been true, as the notoriety of the band only escalated as the stories surrounding these incidents were propagated. But above and beyond the obvious discomfort of the individual victims, these pranks broke the old taboo against journalists becoming part of the story; as the News Of The World used to say at the end of every exposé, *"we made our excuses and left."* This taboo was itself erected to maintain the binary hierarchical relationship between the observer and the observed, and like all status binaries it was dangerous to ignore, because doing so in this case challenged the legitimacy of the music press as a whole. If journalists were incapable of objectively observing, then they garnered no special status in attempting to do so; therefore the only effective way that the press could respond to The Stranglers' provocations was to progressively isolate and ignore them. Whether good or bad, all publicity comes with consequences.

No More Heroes repeated the success of *Rattus Norvegicus*, reaching the No.2 spot in the album charts, and remaining in them for a total of 18 weeks. The release marked a creative hiatus, as the usable material that the group had accumulated over the embryonic stage of their career was now almost exhausted. For the first time, The Stranglers would have to generate a suite of new songs from scratch – to write to order – and the radical direction they were about to take was presaged by a song that emerged from the *Heroes* sessions. "In The Shadows" was released as the B-side of the "No More Heroes" single, over the protests of producer Martin Rushent, who deplored what he saw as its self-indulgence and lack of commercial appeal. However, with its sinister dub-spacey ambience, spidery guitar, wraithlike keyboards and ominous, trepidatious bass, it was a window into the future. Unheralded, its evocation of pervasive urban dread laid the template for post-punk.

The band were packed off to Bearshanks Lodge, a farm near Oundle in rural Northamptonshire, owned by Ruan O'Lochlainn, a musician friend of the band's manager Dai Davies, for two snowbound months during the winter of 1977-78 to write and rehearse new material. As well as the music for the group's next album, a side effect of the band's isolation was the revelation of Jet Black's interest in UFOs, as he had brought along his subscription copies of *Flying Saucer Review* to wile away any spare time. As Hugh Cornwell was to relate to Gary Kent:

We became aware of the fact that Jet was reading these UFO magazines, and he explained to me the whole idea about these UFO's, and I said to John and Dave: 'You gotta listen to this, it's amazing what Jet's reading – it would make an amazing album.' Everyone got into it, the idea of the Meninblack.

At the same time another, apparently simultaneous, notion was hatched in their minds:

We were very frustrated at being labeled by so many journalists and none of these labels we were very happy with. Out of that came the idea of not wearing any colours, so by wearing black, we wouldn't be giving any indications by our clothes.

It is somewhat odd that the group thought that both these ideas, of The Meninblack and The Men In Black, were unrelated, and just happened to arrive concurrently, as they were clearly intimately linked. The extraterrestrial Meninblack were in reality an externalised abstraction of the dangerous, liminal currents present within the ambiguous structure of the band itself, and the negative effects that The Stranglers believed the aliens had on their career were to a great extent representations of their own self-destructive tendencies. The Meninblack were a reflexive phenomenon, and the group's failure to realise this meant that they had no control over them.

Notable also was that in identifying with the colour black, they had also identified with the inferior element of the white/black status binary, a binary they explicitly acknowledged with the title of their third album, *Black And White*, which they recorded at TW Studios during February 1978, and released on March 12th. Expectations were so high that there were 134,000 advance orders for the record, though what the fans were about to receive was going to be a forbidding departure from The Stranglers' previous work.

The sleeve picture, taken by Ruan O'Lochlainn at Bearshanks, depicted the group set against a stark white background, which signified the snowbound conditions in which the music was written. It also signified the blinding flash of a nuclear explosion, and a new drug that had been added to the group's narcotic inventory: cocaine, which now supplemented their staple diet of hashish and LSD. Conceptually, the record was divided between a White side and a Black side. The original intention was for one side to be comprised purely of Cornwell songs, and the other to be reserved for ones by Burnel, with one side being pressed in white vinyl and the other black. Neither idea proved possible in practice, so it was only the labels that were different colours, while each side was merely biased to either of the two main writers.

Sonically, the record was unprecedented. Gone was the warm, sleazy throb of the first two LPs, and in its place was a kind of glacial muscularity. The band had taken two of their key influences, the spaciousness of dub reggae, and the arhythmic terseness of Captain Beefheart, and fused them together in a disturbing new compound. Certainly, a similar kind of dread-invoking space had been anticipated by avant-gardists such as Cabaret Voltaire and Pere Ubu, but The Stranglers were unique in giving this sound a real sense of oppressive mass.

With *Black And White* The Stranglers had successfully abstracted their sound. Dave Greenfield's Hammond keyboards, increasingly fed through the Mini Moog, had lost much of their melodicism, and become spectral and ambient. Cornwell's guitar started to meander into a cat's cradle of sound. Jet Black's drumming became less linear and more structural, opening up the spaces for the other instruments to drift through. The one instrument whose presence didn't attenuate was Burnel's bass, which became even more brutally dominant, its tone channeling deeper into the listener's marrow. This awesome, hideous sound, whose nadir has never really been equalled, largely manufactured itself, as Cornwell was to explain:

The reason it occurred in the first place was because John had a speaker cabinet that was about the size of a door with 16 or so ten-inch speakers, which are a bit small to be taking bass. They all blew one after the other, so he ended up with a huge bass cabinet with blown speakers, but the sound got dirtier and dirtier, and became a feature of the band.

This corrupted, subterranean tumult arouses deep disquiet in the listener, and as such evokes a feeling that the German religious scholar Rudolf Otto identified as Holy Dread. Otto believed that religious feeling, a sense of what he called "the numinous", evolved from primeval man's experience of the "uncanny", that borderline area that abuts the supernatural, and which evolves in mature religious form into the irrational co-existence of God's goodness and God's wrath. Both Sigmund Freud and Emile Durkheim also recognised this duality; that the taboos that surrounded the divine reached out in two directions – that of the sacred and that of the profane – and that each had a contagious quality that could pollute the other, inevitably summoning the irrational, destructive forces of the supernatural. When rock music is at its most anti-structural, it also tends to evoke this ambiguous feeling of wonder-dread, and indeed that is a large part of the music's appeal – it reacquaints us with that magical sense of the power of the numinous that the disenchantment of the world has attempted to eliminate. However, the danger to the musicians themselves, devoid of the ritual precautions undertaken by those who professionally interact with the supernatural, is considerable. The sound that The Stranglers were evolving was a manifestation of their ever-deeper immersion into the numinous.

Lyrically too, the group had widened their horizons, their concerns on the album focusing on the related issues of the ever-increasing encroachment of technology in daily life, and the terrifying implications of technology that underlay the Cold War. Like the sacred, technology also simultaneously reaches out in two directions; in the bureaucratising inclination to proscribe and limit human spontaneity, and in the granting to mankind of superhuman powers of extension and destruction. And both of these, following Ellul, are aspects of the city's tendencies towards slavery and warfare.

The scorching opening track on the LP, "Tank" sardonically exults in the Promethean powers granted by modern weaponry:

Can you see the bullet's high velocity
It can blow a man's arm off at the count of three
If I get my hands on one of those I'm something to watch out for

The song highlights the strange paradox of the individual in the Army, being granted the godlike ability to apportion life or death, while at the same time being mercilessly restricted by regimentation. Hence the strange aura of irrationality that always appends itself to the military, and that found its ultimate expression in the Cold War doctrine of Mutually Assured Destruction, a kind of stand-off between exterminating angels. Cornwell detected an unusual affinity between the military and the music industry, as he explained in *Song By Song*:

> We'd done a lot of touring and I saw a similarity between being on the road and belonging to a military organisation. The last verse is very much about being on tour. I always used to send cards home to my parents, telling them where I was.

The next song, "Nice 'n' Sleazy", the only single to be taken from the album, was something of a throwback to the innuendo-laden fare of the first two LPs, and was another allusion to the band's experiences with the Amsterdam chapter of the Hells Angels. The title, being a parody of Frank Sinatra's "Nice 'n' Easy", briefly attracted the attention of the American crooner's lawyers. Malcolm McLaren recognised a good idea when he heard it, and had Sid Vicious releasing his version of "My Way" a couple of months later. In the September of 1978, "Nice 'n' Sleazy" would earn supreme notoriety when the band performed it alongside a troupe of strippers at their headline concert in Battersea Park, an event that confirmed the band's utter incorrigibility in the minds of the music press, who pruriently splashed as many photos of the disgraceful event as they could over their news pages. The NME in particular would subject their male adolescent readership to an unending cavalcade of pictures of the cavorting young ladies, no doubt leaving them suitably educated and chastened.

This exuberance is quickly diffused by perhaps the most

sober and profound song on the album, "Outside Tokyo", a waltz-time piece that laments the invention of clock time. In doing so it is the first explicit expression of Cornwell's under-lying animus towards the forces of bureaucratic rationalisation, because as Lewis Mumford was to point out in *Technics And Civilisation*, "*the clock is not merely a means of keeping track of the hours, but of synchronizing the actions of men.*" In the opening verse Cornwell identified the link between mechanical time and industrialism:

Somewhere outside Tokyo invented time
Someone in a factory invented time

Mumford believed that the mechanical clock was the key device behind the disenchantment of the world. It was the paradigmatic machine that enabled the invention of all the others, marking "*a perfection toward which other machines aspire*", and placing an abstract grid over biological time, in turn forcing humans to adopt strange, unnatural patterns of behaviour. It compelled man to wake earlier and sleep later, synchronised his actions with those of others in the division of labour, and, what Ellul called its "*knife-edge divisions*", allowed his movements and motions to be analyzed and manipulated in terms of their productive efficiency, a process that saw its ultimate expression in Taylorism. As Mumford was to explain:

The clock ... is a piece of power-machinery whose 'product' is seconds and minutes: by its essential nature it dissociated time from human events and helped create the belief in an independent world of mathematically measurable sequences: the special world of science. There is relatively little foundation for this belief in common human experience: throughout the year the days are of uneven duration ... in terms of the human organism itself, mechanical time is even more foreign: while human life has regularities of its own, the beat of the pulse, the breathing of the lungs, these change from hour to hour with mood and action, and in the longer span of days, time is measured not by the calendar, but by the events that occupy it.

The tyrannical regime of the clock is modern man's greatest oppressor, and yet has come to be assumed as so normal that its pernicious influence largely goes unnoticed. Yet such a bizarrely compulsive time-sensibility was unprecedented in human history. Oswald Spengler compared the Western conception of time with that of the Classical Greek, noting:

Till the epoch of Pericles, the time of day was estimated merely by the length of shadow ... prior to that there was no exact subdivision of the day ... it is a bizarre, but nevertheless psychologically exact, fact that the Hellenic physics ... neither knew the use nor felt the absence of the time-element, whereas we on the other hand work in thousands of a second.

Lewis Mumford observed that, up to the thirteenth century, the pressure for the development of the mechanical clock, which would become the midwife for the rationalising science that would eventually sideline God, came from the monks of Benedictine monasteries, who needed a means to mark the Canonical Hours that had been decreed by Pope Sabanianus. The strange paradox of mechanical time was that it evolved from a religious impulse to posit a mechanical universe in which God was an external director, and the Church his only interpolator, so as to counter the animist idea of Him being immanent in nature and accessible to heretics. But the mechanical science that the Catholic Church instigated would eventually attempt to remove God, and the supernatural in general, from the universe as an unnecessary hypothesis. The unnoticed danger, as we have seen, is that the supernatural does not go away.

And so the forlorn Hugh Cornwell recognises that, due to the new industrial powerhouse of Japan with its *"50 million watches with a strap to sell"*, the reign of rationalism can only become more despotic still. All he can do is console himself with a lullaby:

> *If they should ever sell out*
> *That would be the end of*
> *Be the end of*
> *Be the end of time*

Following this, "Sweden (All Quiet On The Eastern Front)" was a mordant appraisal of the land that had nurtured Cornwell's antinomianism. The Apollonian sense of neatness and order that pervaded Sweden seems to have disturbed the singer profoundly. As he was to tell Jim Drury:

> *The Swedish authorities had amazing powers and it was quite remarkable the way the population obeyed them … There was this state control going on all the time and I found that a bit disquieting.*

It was the apparently benign nature of that Scandinavian nation's orderliness that Cornwell found most perturbing; the authorities made helpful suggestions that were designed to promote wellbeing, such as turning on vehicle fog-lights when visibility was reduced, and the population passively obeyed. Alcohol was also restricted for the benefit of social order:

> *It was quite remarkable, having to show your identity card to purchase alcohol. There was also a restriction on how much alcohol you could buy every month.*

Cornwell's aversion to Sweden recalls the work of the German esoteric philosopher Rudolf Steiner, and his idea that there were two mutually opposing poles of evil, which he called "Ahriman" and "Lucifer". Ahriman is the concept of evil that we are most familiar with; that of the coarse, compulsive need for material wealth and sensual experience, regardless of the consequences for self or others. Lucifer, on the other hand, is the vice of spiritual pride and the sense of superiority that results from self-denial and altruism; the belief that being able to rise above the corruption of the world makes one too good for it.

For Cornwell, Sweden was a kind of Luciferian hell, its progressive "Nordic model" of egalitarian social democracy a foretaste of the ultimate destiny of the rationalisation of the world, where the crooked timber of humanity is finally levelled straight. It was boringly perfect, drearily bereft of spontaneity and impropriety, with all vices permitted but carefully circum-scribed and rationed. Big Brother may have said it was the place to go, but the oppression the Swedish Big Brother subjected its populace to was that of incontestable good manners and common sense. Indeed, pious, risk-averse Nordic Luciferism has since infected the rest of the Western world, much to the delight of its bourgeois liberals.

As we have seen though, Sweden had its dark, irrational side, and The Stranglers were to collide with a particularly virulent manifestation of it during their *No More Heroes* tour in September 1977. The Stockholm University riots of the 1950s may have given birth to the "rebels without a cause", but that decade also gave birth to another American-influenced subculture at the other end of the social spectrum. The Raggare were rural working-class youths who were brought together by their enthusiasm for hot-rodding imported American cars, but they soon gave rise to a full-blown moral panic that only accelerated in the ensuing decades due to their aggressive stance towards other youth cults. Dismissive of hippies, they were openly violent towards Punks, and the Sex Pistols had been involved in a fracas with the Raggare during their tour of Sweden a couple of months earlier.

When the unsuspecting Stranglers arrived for what they thought would be a particularly uneventful concert in a chalet on the outskirts of the small town of Klippan, they were unaware that this apparently anonymous town was a Raggare stronghold, and that the Raggare themselves viewed their presence as a deliberate provocation.

Just as the group were setting up their equipment, several hundred Raggare arrived in their convertibles, brandishing chainsaws and other weaponry, and proceeded to destroy the The Stranglers' equipment and assault their road crew. Some of the group members, along with the remaining crew, responded by hurling improvised molotov cocktails at the Raggare's cars, setting light to several of them. After the smoke had cleared, the police proceeded to escort the band out of Sweden for their own safety. Not for the last time, the group had unconsciously managed to find the precise boundary where order turns to disorder, where Apollo meets Dionysus.

If "Sweden" envisaged a rationalised, technicised future as being one of sterile tedium, then "Hey! (Rise Of The Robots)" did just the reverse. Inspired by Isaac Asimov's "I, Robot", it evoked the sheer chaos of technology with its skittering rhythm and the delinquent saxophone of Laura Logic. In *The Technological Society* Jacques Ellul had observed how both technology and the associated behaviours that it demanded of its users, which he classed together in the term "technique", had what he called a "geometric" vector. By this he meant that all new technologies suggested unanticipated applications, which in turn prompted other, hitherto undreamt of further new technologies. In this sense, the growth of technology and technique is uncontrolled – it spreads in unexpected directions, with no heed to the social or cultural consequences of its propagation. Ellul noted that unlike all previous human civilisations, which tended to proscribe technological innovations if their ruling minorities were unable to intuit the consequences of adopting them, Western civilisation is unique in its reluctance to make any kind of moral appraisal of technologies and their associated techniques. Whether technological progress puts thousands, even millions, of people out of work; whether it pollutes the atmosphere; whether it enables the nuclear destruction of entire cities; all this is immaterial when weighed against the faith that technological progress is ultimately benign. It is the naivety of this faith in such an amoral force that led Oswald Spengler to classify Western civilisation as "Faustian".

As a phenomenon that is detached from human control, technology is also therefore fertile ground for paranoia. It is one of the "hidden" forces that shapes individual destinies, but is rarely recognised as such. Military and surveillance technologies; techniques for processing criminals and dissidents; sophisticated methods of advertising and propaganda; these are all products of, and further influences on, the wider network of technological innovation, and yet so insidious are they, and so greatly do they atomise the individual, that it is hard to believe that they are not the products of the most fiendishly intricate plans.

What "Hey! (Rise Of The Robots)" does recognise is that technologies developed by human minds to facilitate human desires, both conscious and unconscious, will ultimately replicate the flawed and contradictory nature of humanity. After a period as uncomplaining servants, Cornwell anticipates that the robots will resort to the familiar industrial strife that afflicted the Britain of the 1970s:

They're gonna want a union soon
Oil break that's dead on noon

Ultimately, robots will suffer the same fate as the men who built the Tower of Babel. Their speech will be confounded; they will leave off the building of their own city.

"Toiler On The Sea" was a thematic departure, and would

introduce a theme that would prove to be oddly salvational for both Cornwell and the band as a whole; that of finding refuge in the womb of narcotised love, in this case in the metaphor of a "woman ship" whose cavernous hull protects an old sea lag from the stormiest waters. The song was inspired by a disastrous trip to Morocco that Cornwell had taken with his girlfriend during a Christmas break from the Bearshank Lodge sessions. Arriving to find that the hotel they were supposed to stay in didn't exist, they were subsequently robbed, contracted food poisoning, and even missed their flight home. Amazingly, Cornwell dumped his girlfriend after this episode as he suspected her of being a jinx, but of course the reverse was true. The trickster phenomenon that was slowly seeping into the group's collective psychology was simply demonstrating that unlike the individual band members themselves, it didn't take time off for vacations. The Morocco fiasco was a foretaste of the calamities that would plague the band during their foreign excursions over the next couple of years.

The bass-heavy, Burnel-dominated "Black" side of the album kicked off with "Curfew", whose disorienting structure, featuring three different time signatures and bars with missing beats, reflects its nightmarish subject – a Soviet invasion of Britain:

The enemy has cut down all of the power
London south of the Thames is invaded
Westminster is razed down to the ground
The government has fled for Scotland today

The verses are delivered as though in a series of final radio messages, such as were no doubt heard in Budapest in 1956 and Prague in 1968 before the men from the Steppes delivered their vacuum, while the chorus addresses the disconcerting effects of an established social structure being dissolved in an instant:

Grey becomes black and white
Is it true what they say?
They turn the day into night

The inverted structure of the Warsaw Pact, born in opposition to Western Democracy, offers *"a new kind of freedom"*, Erich Fromm's "positive freedom" – an authoritarianism that expunges the ennui and anxiety that pervades life in the West by mandating how to think and act. *"Freedom's a chain"* sings Burnel ambivalently, viewing the reversal in circumstances as no worse than the self-indulgent, libertarian "negative freedom" of the American Dream.

"Threatened" and "In The Shadows" reveal The Stranglers' sound at its very darkest, what the band dubbed the "Barracuda Bass" very much summoning something hostile and predatory glimmering in the depths. Both songs are hesitantly paced, unsure of what horror is lurking in the darkness beyond vision. "In The Shadows" pulses with the nocturnal terrors of Seventies Britain; the streets of Belfast adulterated with death squads, the cities of the mainland prowling with Rippers and Black Panthers. The song examines the uncanny nature of what Owen Barfield termed "figuration" – that ambivalent process in which external phenomena are resolved into collective representations; when the external world starts to become structured in consciousness:

Is it a dog?
Is it a cat ?
Is it a dog?
What do you think of that?

Nighttime is the period when the human visual representation system is at its least responsive and reliable, and when the mind therefore has the greatest tendency to "fill in the gaps" with the imagination. The increased possibility of genuine danger sharpens the nervous system, projecting threats onto harmless shadows, while real menaces can go unnoticed. There is something genuinely unpalatable following The Stranglers though, something *"moving, shiny, bright"* that cannot yet be identified and classified.

Finally, "Enough Time" brings the record to a close on an appropriately apocalyptic note. The song was ironically titled: it was written in the studio after a demand from Martin Rushent to bring the LP up to the appropriate length, *"bleeding us dry"* as Cornwell would put it. The track itself documents the ultimate horror of rationalism out of control – a nuclear holocaust, with black rain falling from the sky and the seas being sucked away into tsunamis. Burnel's bass creaks and groans like rusting pipelines at the bottom of the ocean. The "four minute warning", the time expected for nuclear warheads launched in Russia to reach the UK, was a commonplace of the Cold War, and insinuated both a liminal feeling of tension and a sense of immediacy to everyday life. After a structured beginning, the song degenerates into a miasma of noise, as though the crust of the planet is disintegrating, before a Morse-coded message, foregrounded in the mix, rings out to the beings of another planet:

SOS. THIS IS PLANET EARTH. WE ARE FUCKED. PLEASE ADVISE.

Then a strange thing happens. Cornwell's vocals slow down, as if the end of time predicted in "Outside Tokyo" is actually arriving. Yet simultaneously, JJ Burnel's voice, fed through a harmoniser, starts to speed up, breaking into a cacophonous, mocking baby-babble that multiplies into the sound of a host. It is the voice of The Meninblack in person, making their first Earthly appearance at the moment of Armageddon. And as this birth in chaos suggests, they do not come in peace. Significantly, both sets of voices are singing the same refrain: *"Have you got enough time?"* confirming that The Meninblack are indeed a projection of The Stranglers themselves.

Black And White repeated the success of its predecessors, going straight to the Number 2 position in the album charts. The first three Stranglers albums would each sell a quarter of million copies in their first year of sale. The album's parched, cocaine-induced dryness deeply impressed the disc jockey John Peel, who played the entire album in one sitting on his Radio One evening show.

The press release for the new LP had been held at an unusual location – Rejkjavik in Iceland – and it included a gig at the national Exhibition Centre. The harsh, monochrome landscape of that frozen volcanic island was judged by the group to offer an appropriate metaphor for their new, attenuated sound. As usual, where The Stranglers led their peers would follow, with other post-punk luminaries arriving in Iceland in their wake, including The Fall, Killing Joke and Echo & The Bunnymen; and, equally predictably, the Men In Black's trailblazing would eventually be written out of history.

In a certain respect, the marginalisation of The Stranglers paid dividends for the punk movement as a whole, as it opened up a space in which other groups could adopt their oeuvre almost as a kit of parts to construct their own identities. Pitch-black bass used as a lead instrument, angular Beefheartian guitar, crepuscular synths, and light, hesitant drumming became de rigeur, as did the themes of urban desolation, technological encroachment, paranoia and the Cold War. Albums such as Joy Division's *Unknown Pleasures* and Public Image Limited's *Metal Box* would garner plaudits for musical innovations that "In The Shadows" had conceived a full two years earlier. Indeed *Unknown Pleasures* even replicated the white side/black side conceptual scheme. Sometimes the influence of The Stranglers was even more direct – Hugh Cornwell paid for the first demo session of the Bristol punk-funkers The Pop Group, though they had enough nous not to make the mistake of thanking him publicly.

The *Black And White* sessions did yield another, non-album single, the band's cover version of the Bacharach and David classic, "Walk On By", although its sales potential was impaired by the fact that the group had already given away an extended version of the song as a free gift with the first 75,000 copies of the album. Whereas the celebrated Dionne Warwick recording expressed the selfless wish to bear the suffering of a relationship break-up alone, The Stranglers homed in on the miniscule speck of resentment that underlay Warwick's performance and amplified it into a festering sneer of self-pity and self-loathing, utterly inverting the noble sentiments of the original. *"All the tears and the sadness YOU gave me"* sang the bitter, accusatory Hugh Cornwell.

The B-side, "Old Codger" was equally arresting, a collaboration with the jazz singer and critic George Melly, one of the band's very few media allies. Melly himself was no stranger to outrage, with his bisexuality and raucous stage presence, and was thus a perfect foil for The Stranglers. Before his musical career he had almost been court-martialed for distributing anarchist literature while serving in the Royal Navy, an organisation he had only joined, according to his autobiography *Rum, Bum and Concertina*, because he liked the uniforms. As an art critic, Melly was fascinated by the disruptive movements of the early twentieth century, particularly the Surrealists, whose use of incongruous juxtapositions undermined the precise definition of objective reality inherent in Enlightenment rationalism. Melly had been much taken with the hysteria that The Stranglers engendered, and had asked them to make a cameo appearance in a documentary he was making about Dadaism for the BBC's *Arena* arts programme. Melly shrewdly identified the group as *"heirs to Dada"*, and understood that their antagonism was fundamental to their being, rather than just their act. The band returned the favour by writing "Old Codger" for him, a song

4

about an ageing *debauchee* which he attacked with a gleeful, saucy vigour, to the blistering harmonica accompaniment of Canvey Island bluesman and occasional jailbird Lew Lewis.

A couple of successful tours with the new material from *Black And White* were to be rounded off in October with a prestigious concert at Surrey University in Guildford, which was to be televised by the BBC as an episode of their *Rock Goes To College* series. As a condition of their appearance, the band had asked their management's PR representative to arrange with the BBC that half the tickets for the concert be sold through the local independent record shop Bonaparte Records, so that their Guildford fanbase would be given a chance of attending the gig. On arriving at the University campus they discovered that all the tickets had been given away to students as part of fresher's week, some of them during a cheese and wine party. When evening came, enquiries conducted among the throng queuing to get in revealed that they were almost all students, with the small number of genuine fans having to pay over the odds for a ticket. The Stranglers managed to sneak in a few locals, but on discovering that these had been subsequently ejected by the stewards, and feeling that they had been tricked by the BBC and the University, they quickly improvised a plan to scupper the recording.

The schedule for the concert was for the group to perform three warm-up numbers while the BBC's Outside Broadcasting unit could check the sound levels and camera positions, and fix any possible technical problems, and then they would be re-introduced for the televised performance. The Stranglers used the intervals between these three songs to berate the audience. After "Ugly" and "I Feel Like A Wog", Hugh told the heaving throng:

This is fucking boring. You lot are a load of the most boring people I've ever seen in my fucking life. Nube count's pretty low as well. You all look like fresher girls.

While Burnel announced *"Will all the students please go home."*

"Bring On The Nubiles" was followed by some class-conscious enquiries from Cornwell:

Anyone from Bellfields Estate here? Never heard of it have you? Two people. Anyone from Park Barn? Three people. Jesus!

Jet Black then asked *"Anyone from Guildford University?"* After a roar from the crowd he replied *"Fuck Off!"*

The cameras were then turned on for "Burning Up Time", and host Pete Drummond returned to introduce the band for the viewers at home. Referencing a popular children's television programme of the time, Cornwell asked the audience *"have you all got your Crackerjack pencils?"* before offering the terse advice to *"stick them up your arses then."*

A fast pile-driving version of "Hanging Around" was followed by Cornwell's announcement:

Guildford University never represented Guildford. We hate playing to elitist audiences, so fuck off!

And the band walked off the stage, ending the televised performance after two numbers. The whole farrago was a stunning moment of career self-sabotage, and marks the moment when The Stranglers truly started to go off the rails. It was to have serious consequences as regards the band's relationship with the BBC, an organisation that was never particularly well disposed towards them in the first place, as the Outside Broadcast manager Michael Appleton would go on to become the producer of *The Old Grey Whistle Test*. This was the Corporations premier "serious" music show, and The Stranglers would consequently never get an invite to appear on it, as Appleton felt that the group had squandered an opportunity that could have been given to another, more appreciative, act.

The Stranglers' ultra-egalitarian attitude was somewhat puzzling, as they were for the most part lower middle class, and Cornwell and Burnel had been students themselves. Nevertheless, their experience of living in Guildford had been one of acute poverty, even if this was to a certain extent self-imposed. The suspicion has to be that the real target of the evening's insubordination was the BBC itself, which was exactly the kind of nebulous, faceless, paternalistic, authoritarian, bureaucratised institution that the group were temperamentally hostile to. As the state broadcaster, the BBC, to use George Hansen's term, is the most powerful "spirit" in Britain; the most effective shaper and maintainer of the invisible hierarchical structure that fixes and conditions British society. There is ever something sinister and ghostly about the Corporation, and this is somehow accentuated by its craving to appear warm and homely, as part of the furniture, as *"Auntie Beeb"*.

The event also highlighted the unpredictable, schizoid nature of The Stranglers. They worked like Stakhanovites for their record company, and had performed on numerous occasions for "Top Of The Pops", committing far less mischief than the BBC had feared. Yet at crucial, and often the most unexpected moments, their behaviour, following internal currents that were opaque from the outside, could be baffling, or terrifying, or a mixture of both.

The farrago at Surrey University would be followed by the first major hiatus in The Stranglers' career, which was only inter-rupted by their first tours of Japan and Australia during the February and March of 1979. During this period JJ Burnel would record his *Euroman Cometh* album, that was released in April 1979, and Hugh Cornwell would conduct a short press tour of Los Angeles, and begin a series of experimental recordings there with his friend Robert Williams, the drummer of Captain Beefheart's Magic Band. These extra-curricular activities were a sign that the band's success was starting to corrode the intense clan-like bonds that had hitherto held them together, and this was to have serious repercussions over the next stage of their career.

The band reunited again in May at an isolated farmhouse in Perugia, Italy, owned by the father of Burnel's then girlfriend, to write material for their next album. This was a far more idyllic location than Bearshanks Lodge had been, and marked a moment of calm before the maelstrom that was about to hit the group. They then relocated to EMI's Pathe Marconi studios in Paris to begin recording, either because, according to Cornwell, TW Studios had closed, or, according to Burnel, to save on tax. Burnel, with his belief that the nation state was an outmoded institution, could no doubt have generated an ideological reason for any tax avoidance, but the fact was that The Stranglers had become a more substantial organisation, with a more unwieldy agglomeration of equipment and a dedicated road crew on paid retainers, all of which increased their overheads. Another, unstated reason for the move to France may have been that the band's record company, United Artists, had been acquired by EMI, who would the following year reassign all the former UA-signed artists to the revived Liberty label.

The first fruits of the Paris sessions were released in August 1979 with "Duchess", an unusually breezy, bouncy pop single about an aristocratic girlfriend of Cornwell's who lived in a terraced house in Chelsea and claimed lineage to Henry VIII. The humorous video, which featured the band dressed as choirboys in mirror shades crooning in a church was banned by the BBC for being blasphemous, it is alleged at the instigation of no less a person than Cliff Richard. "Duchess" may have been a commercial success, reaching a respectable Number 14 in the singles chart, but was as uncharacteristic of the forthcoming long player as "Nice 'n' Sleazy" had been of Black And White. It was the record's B-side that was to give more indication of the trouble that lay ahead. "Fool's Rush Out" was a bitter farewell to the band's management team of Derek Savage and Dai Davies, who had called a meeting with the band after the release of *Black And White*, and, after informing them that they had gone too far in their provocations, suggested that they follow the example of the Sex Pistols, and split up. As Cornwell was to inform Jim Drury:

They said it would be counter-productive for us to carry on. You must remember by this point the Pistols had split up, so the force behind punk had disintegrated and everything was moving into new styles. So Dai and Derek thought the best thing would be to split up and possibly reform down the line.

This open declaration of a lack of confidence in The Stranglers from the two men who the group had considered as mentors was to have a profound effect on the band. One result was the decision by the two frontmen to pursue side projects partly as insurance against the disintegration of the group. Although their management team's booker, Ian Grant, would step into the breach and become their new manager, the decision of the shrewd pairing of Savage and Davies to bail out was surely a bad omen. It was apparent that they had joined the growing number of music industry insiders who viewed the band as a bad proposition.

After playing only new material during a support slot for The Who later in August, a typically risky move, The Strangler's fourth album, *The Raven* was released the following month, and marked another evolution in the band's music and worldview. The record began with two Viking-themed tracks, the brief instrumental "Longships", followed by the epic title track, and this theme is replicated with the painting of a raven on the front cover, and the back cover photograph of the band in a recon-structed longship, the "Hugin", that is located in Pegwell Bay in Kent. Burnel was to state that the raven iconography was drawn from Norse mythology, in which Hugin ("mind") and Munin ("memory") are a pair of ravens that circumnavigate the Earth and bring back information to the king of the gods, Odin, and that with the new album the band themselves were bringing back the information they had garnered from their experiences touring abroad.

The symbolism of Odin, Hugin and Munin is intriguing, as Odin himself had a dual-identity, as the god of war, hunting and death, and yet also as the god of magic, poetry and prophecy. He also kept two wolves known as Geri and Freki who were eternally ravenous, and in this respect he recalls the Greek god Apollo, for whom both wolves and ravens were sacred. There is clearly a connection with prehistoric totemism in these relationships, and, as we shall see, an understanding of totemism is vital to explaining how the Trickster constellation manifests itself.

"Dead Loss Angeles" is the first report from the far corners of the Earth, and was inspired by Hugh Cornwell's visits to L.A. to write and record with Robert Williams. The song, with its twin bass lines, one played by Cornwell, evokes the city as an utterly alien place, a *"lunar base camp"* full of *"android Americans"*. Cornwell's deathly, deadpan delivery is utterly underwhelmed by these artificial, inorganic surroundings. As he opined in *Song By Song*:

L.A. is an old fishing village, but there's no real reason for it to exist anymore. It feels like a temporary place, that you could look out of your window and see everything gone.

Cornwell revealed another source of inspiration in the work of the science fiction writers Harlan Ellison and Philip K. Dick, whose books *"were full of conspiracies and deceptions where the world of the future was set up to trick people."* It is notable for Cornwell to name-check Dick in particular, as this writer was notorious for evolving a byzantine personal theology that foreshadowed The Stranglers' own Meninblack concept.

Dick had experienced a bizarre psychological episode during

February and March 1974, which he thereafter referred to as 2-3-74, after returning home from a visit to his dentist, during which he had been given an injection of sodium pentathol. He underwent a series of hypnagogic hallucinations, some of which lasted all night long and which he was to later describe as a theophany, a direct appearance of God. Over the following years he would attempt to explain these experiences in a sprawling private work called "Exegesis", and his conclusions would inform much of his fiction. He evolved a belief system in which the Earth was the Black Iron Prison (BIP) ruled by a sinister authoritarian cabal known as "Empire", of whom Richard Nixon was a signal example. This conspiratorial grouping was allowed to function through the human tendency towards amnesia, whose inhibiting effect prevents mankind from achieving communication with VALIS (Vast Active Living Intelligence System), a satellite that orbited the Earth, and was operated by extra-terrestrials from the "Dog Star" Sirius, in the constellation Canis Major. Dick believed that the theophanies he experienced were due to VALIS utilising "disinhibiting stimuli" to communicate with him, triggering the recollection of "intrinsic knowledge" through the removal of amnesia, and thereby achieving spiritual enlightenment, or "gnosis." This gnosis included the revelation that the universe was purely comprised of information, and that the phenomenal world that we experience was purely an illusion, a cage formed from our own forgetfulness.

Dick had constructed a novel, modern version of an old metaphysical idea, that of Gnosticism. In place of the traditional monistic Christian conception of all Creation being the work of the one true God, Gnosticism posited the dualistic idea that the Earth, the imperfect, ephemeral world associated with matter, flesh and time, was created by a false God, known as the "Demiurge", and ruled by his underlings known as "Archons". The remote "upper world" of the true God was located outside this "lower world" and could only be accessed by "gnosis": the garnering of hidden spiritual knowledge that allowed access to the divine. The Stranglers' own Meninblack theology adopted elements of Gnostic thought, especially the idea of the Earth being a fallen world – a corrupt, irredeemable prison. However, the band omitted the transcendental element, so that there was no liberating knowledge to be obtained in their universe. It was Gnosticism without the gnosis. All the group could offer in compensation was an individual orientation to this sordid reality. For Burnel, it was phlegmatic temperament of the warrior – meeting life's vicissitudes like the Viking or the Samurai. For Cornwell, it was a retreat into the womb-like reveries offered by drugs and sexual love.

The exquisite "Baroque Bordello" was just such an evocation of the boudoir as a protective *"walnut shell"*. A strong candidate for being the band's greatest song, it had an unusual structure in which Cornwell and Burnel play in different time signatures, 7/8 against 4/4, with the two coinciding every 14 bars. One of the general side effects of the Meninblack obsession was that The Stranglers seemed to lose the ability to pick their best singles, and "Baroque Bordello" was passed over in favour of the song that followed it on the LP, "Nuclear Device". Subtitled "The Wizard Of Aus", the song was inspired by their chaotic tour of Australia, which had stood in stark contrast to the respectful welcome they had encountered in Japan.

The Wizard Of Aus in question was Joh Bjelke-Petersen, the premier of the state of Queensland, and one of the most notorious politicians in Australian history. This Lutheran ultra-conservative, who believed God had chosen him to save Australia from socialism, was almost like an Archon made flesh. He managed to remain in office for nearly 20 years, despite his National Party never winning a majority share of votes, due to an inherent bias in the state electoral system that apportioned a greater weighing to rural votes. After becoming Premier in 1971, Bjelke-Petersen gradually turned Queensland into a virtual police state, with public protests banned, trade unionists dismissed from public posts, and aboriginal land rights overturned in the interests of mining and oil drilling companies. He also exhibited a strong puritanical streak by banning Playboy magazine, opposing school sex education, and prohibiting condom vending machines. His dislike of "southern homosexuals" and the (conservative) Liberal Prime Minister Malcolm Fraser eventually led him to propose Queensland secede from Australia and establish its own currency.

Bjelke-Petersen's government was also institutionally corrupt, and regularly turned a blind eye to police violence and malpractice. The Stranglers arrived in the state capital of Brisbane, shortly after an appearance on the early evening Channel 7 television show *Willesee At 7*, during which they advocated the use of drugs and swore at the presenter, a performance that had the same kind of effect as the Sex Pistols' interview with Bill Grundy back home. Their gig in the city was infiltrated by Bjelke-Petersen's supporters, and a fight was deliberately provoked in the audience in order to get the gig stopped and the venue closed down. In the melee, Cornwell's head was gashed with a beer mug. A subsequent concert in Adelaide, South Australia, was attended by the local police, who then raided the band's hotel room, although they found, to their chagrin, no incriminating behaviour.

"Nuclear Device" describes one of Bjelke-Petersen's more bizarre schemes, to build a Uranium enrichment plant in the south-east of Queensland, which was only rumoured at the time, but subsequent document releases have revealed was a real project. The song imagines the Queensland Premier's lust for power lurching into megalomania, but it is the song's spoken-word closing refrain that brings the actions of this seeming eccentric into the wider Stranglers worldview, connecting as it does the repression of the Australian state with the obedient orderliness of Sweden:

Getting rid of Abo's one by one
Buy cheap land for uranium
It reminds me of Sweden
Got the same sort of freeze on

There is then a connection with the Meninblack, as Cornwell fancies the strange marsupial fauna of Down Under as being the result of long-ago nuclear experiments conducted by other-worldly beings. It is the first indication that the Meninblack concept is also a creation myth:

All the animals look so strange
All victims of a testing range

The first song on the second side of the album addresses another sinister Archon lording it over a powerful energy source – the Shah of Iran, who *"sold the English all their oil"* and *"made the people work the soil"*. Unlike Bjelke-Petersen, however, Shah Mohammad Reza Pahlavi had already seen his reign toppled by the Ayatollah Khomeini, the severe Islamic cleric who had fomented unrest from his Paris exile by distributing his sermons on cheap cassette tapes. This was an example of technology being utilised in the dissemination of traditionalist, anti-modern ideas, and demonstrated once again how technology could easily be used for perverse, unanticipated ends.

The Iranian Revolution was an enormous shock to the West, unleashing the second great oil crisis of the decade, and humiliating the USA, which had to watch impotently as its Tehran embassy staff were held hostage for 444 days. The Stranglers looked to Nostradamus for guidance, and printed a translation of his Quatrain number 70 on the inner sleeve of the album:

Rain, famine and war will not cease in Persia:
too great a faith will betray the monarch.

Those (actions) started in France will end there,
a secret sign for one to be sparing.

The Shah, whose reign was noted for its callous opulence in a country that suffered from dire extremes of poverty, ruled during the 1953 coup that had overthrown Iran's democratically elected Prime Minister Mohammad Mosaddeq. This coup had been engineered by the US Central Intelligence Agency on behalf of the British secret service department MI6, who had resented Mosaddeq's nationalisation of the British-controlled Anglo-Persian Oil Company, and feared that his reliance on pro-Soviet political parties would see him turn towards the USSR. Indeed the Soviet Union had also been meddling in Iranian internal affairs, having sponsored revolts by ethnic Kurds and Azerbaijanis in the north of the country to support its own demands for a petroleum concession.

A largely unacknowledged side-effect of intelligence agencies such as the CIA, MI6 and the Soviet KGB, engaged in the secretive undermining of foreign governments and other nefarious activities, was to provide an explanatory mechanism for the conspiracy theories that would envelop the Cold War era and beyond. The secret intelligence agencies were, and are, voluminous generators of paranoia, and, as will become apparent, they are also therefore significant instigators of paranormal activity. The ultimate effect on the innocent bystander of their dubious work was ably conveyed by Cornwell himself:

I remember sitting in cars waiting for things to happen, convinced that the end of the world was coming. At the time, there was an oil crisis which could have led to the breakdown of Western society.

"Shah Shah A Go Go" presents a vision of the queer, labyrinthine connections that support and undergird both Western society and the global economy. The West's Promethean powers of economic might and military strength are dependent on a single, terrifyingly finite energy source; that of oil. This dependency is the locus of the most intense activity by the world's intelligence agencies – organisations whose very modus operandi is deception. This in turn gives international affairs a patina of the unreal. Bizarre, unexpected events such as the Iranian Revolution erupt, and the task of interpretation immediately becomes occult; an attempt to piece together multiple hidden and crisscrossing trails. It is just as realistic to consult Nostradamus.

The inner sleeve of *The Raven* also included a newspaper cutting of Iran's new clerical rulers banning all forms of music *"from Beethoven to the Beatles"* as it was *"like opium"*. It quoted the Ayatollah Khomeini as opining *"it stupifies a person listening, and makes the brain active and frivolous"*. However, as the next song on the record was to infer, The Stranglers' introduction to opium was anything but frivolous. It was to be the next step on their journey to ruin.

"Don't Bring Harry" was morbid and funereal, the leaden cascade of the piano melody suggesting the repeating cycle of addiction. It comes as a surprise then that JJ Burnel was to suggest that the band's adoption of the drug was deliberate. As he informed John Robb:

The whole band was meant to take heroin for whole year and see what we would produce at the end of it. Jet and Dave were smart and they got off after a couple of weeks whilst Hugh and I got into it for a whole year and it wasn't that easy giving up but we did eventually. Heroin anaesthetizes you. It desensitizes you so you become less considerate towards other people and a lot more introverted because the only thing that is important is more heroin.

There was a sombre grandeur to the song, a European feel that evoked the grey, oppressive skies and deserted walkways of

Paris in autumn. Heroin was to cast a dark pall over the group, both psychologically and literally in the case of their relationship to authority. If there was one thing that was going to be worse for them than smack however, it was the Meninblack, and on *The Raven* they announced themselves openly.

"Meninblack" once more featured Burnel's voice fed through the harmoniser to create a hideous host, and fleshed out, so to speak, their grotesque creation myth, which linked UFOs to cannibalism. The aliens implanted human life on Earth in the ancient past as an experiment in farming:

First we gave you the wheel
Then we made you live to kill
So the best stock will survive
We eat you all alive

Again this is a Gnostic explanation for the destructive behaviour of mankind, but without the redeeming transcendental element. The unrepentantly evil aliens have created an irremediably corrupt planet. The sluggish rhythm track, suggestive of both planets and centuries turning, was created by taking what had been a proposed single recorded at Eden Studios in late 1978 called "Two Sunspots" and playing the 24-track tape at half-speed. The original vocals were mixed down, and replaced by additional guitar and vocal tracks. The ghoulish result would trigger the departure of Martin Rushent as the band's producer, as he wanted no part in this kind of experimentalism. In his absence the group's former recording engineer Alan Winstanley would become the LP's producer. Rushent was the latest important and experienced ally to jump ship, and yet The Stranglers themselves once again seemed to be blind to the ramifications of this, and what it portended.

The Raven concluded with perhaps the most ominous track of all, "Genetix". Sung by Dave Greenfield, it presented a chilling vision of the possibilities of genetic engineering, with its *"messing round at playing God"*. "Genetix" is fascinating in the dual-aspect of what it implies; firstly it emphasizes the Faustian, geometric aspects of technology – like nuclear fission, once genetic engineering has been made possible it is out of control, as there will always be men who will utilise its ability to grant them power regardless of the collective good. Secondly, the possibilities it opened fed into the group's own Meninblack mythos, as it offered a "rational" explanation for ancient legends and religious lore. In a radio interview with Tim Sommer, Burnel described how the quasi-human creatures of Greek myth, the Centaurs and Minotaurs, could be the results of genetic experiments, and how the Genesis myth of Eve being created from Adam's rib could be an instance of DNA being extracted from bone marrow. He went on to explain:

It's not so wonderful now to think of the Immaculate Conception, because the Immaculate Conception could be artificial insemination.

The song ended with Cornwell narrating the founder of genetic science Gregor Mendel's laws of gene segregation in a neutral, deadpan voice, signifying the amoral nature of science; its separation of fact from value. Mendel himself was an Augustinian friar, and another example of religion being a midwife for a rationalising, disenchanting technology, in this case gene manipulation. With "Genetix" The Stranglers were engaged in turning a scientific explanation of the myth of human creation into another, more terrifying myth.

The Raven was once again a commercial success, reaching Number 4 in the UK Albums Chart, although the band were reputedly robbed of the Number 1 slot due to a proportion of its sales being credited to The Police's *Regatta De Blanc*, a record which had yet to be released. This was not only the second time that The Stranglers had been the victims of a compiling error by the BMRB, it was also the second time that The Police had benefited at the band's expense. The Stranglers' abusive attitude to their American record company A&M had ensured that Sting's group, also signed to that label, would be the major beneficiary of A&M's promotional efforts in the USA.

While the band embarked on a UK tour for the album, the first fruits of Cornwell's collaboration with Robert Williams were revealed with the release on the 25th of October of the "White Room" single, a cover of the classic song by Cream. In this new version, the driving rhythm of the original was replaced by a ponderous barbiturate drag, as though the song was being scraped along the tiled floor of an institution. The lyrics, which had been written by the poet Pete Brown, were concerned with rejection and abandonment, but it was an isolated sense of incarceration that Cornwell and Williams were to focus on:

I'll wait in this place where the sun never shines
Wait in this place where the shadows run from themselves

This was to be prophetic. On the 30th of October, The Stranglers played the penultimate gig of *The Raven* tour in Cardiff. The next evening was to be the final gig at the Rainbow theatre in London, and at 3.30 a.m. on the morning of the 1st of November Cornwell and promoter Paul Loasby were driving in a hire-car down the Westway into London when they ventured into a routine police roadblock on Hammersmith Broadway. Eight squad cars manned by around 50 policemen had been parked diagonally across the four-lane road to channel traffic into a single lane, so that each car could be individually inspected.

Cornwell was not immediately recognised, but what attracted the police's attention was the presence of three sixteen-year-old French fans on the back seat who were being given a lift back to London. These teenagers, two boys and a girl, had arrived in Britain on a whim with no money and nowhere to stay, and were being driven to the lodgings of a friend of Cornwell's. The police suspected they were underage, and asked Loasby, the driver, to get out of the car to be frisked. A small sachet of cocaine was discovered in his top pocket, though the constable thought it was heroin, and barked into his radio *"I think you'd better come over, Sarge. I think we've found Harry."*

This was a case of bring on the nubiles, but don't bring Harry. Loasby was taken away for questioning, and Cornwell and the teenagers were then frisked, though nothing was found. Cornwell was about to return to the car to collect his bag, when he saw the vehicle being driven off to the nearest police station. By the time he had walked there to collect it, he knew that the contents of the bag would have been discovered – a gram and a half of cocaine, 90 milligrams of heroin, half an ounce of cannabis resin, a wrap of grass and two packets of magic mushrooms. By no means a large cache, but enough for him to be charged that morning, along with Loasby.

This episode was odd firstly because such sweeps were rare even in the Britain of the late 1970s, when the ever-present threat of Irish Republican terrorism might have given them a basis of justification. More significant though was the eerie way it had been foreshadowed by the moment in Sweden when Cornwell's car had been commandeered for a routine police check while he was smoking cannabis on the back seat. Was that event a warning? Or an omen?

The court hearing was scheduled for the beginning of January 1980, which allowed The Stranglers to go ahead with their scheduled tours of northern Europe and Japan. Their career self-sabotage could also continue unabated, and on the 9th of November they released the "Don't Bring Harry" EP. This was about as perverse a record as could possibly be imagined; an ostensible "Christmas single" released over a month early, that showcased a gloomy song about heroin addiction, played at 33 1/3 rpm, and featured a dead turkey on the cover. The Radio 1 disc jockey Dave Lee Travis took time out to lengthily condemn it on-air.

To spice up the festive mood, the EP also featured "Crabs", Burnel's song about pubic lice, a live version of "In The Shadows", and another Cornwell and Williams composition, the itchy, frantic "Wired". Ostensibly about being on cocaine, "Wired" immerses itself in a world where the machinery has run amok, where the tapes run backwards, and conjures a diorama of technology as a gateway to Hell that even Jacques Ellul would have been proud of:

So what are you on?
An escalator
Taking you underground

There was also an echo here of the condemned man being sent down to the cells, and this was intensified with the release of the song's parent long player a week later. *Nosferatu* was a real dungeon of a record; a spiritual cesspit, replete with oppressive, clanging rhythms and distant whistles and shrieks; the sound of guards strolling past wailing inmates. The original idea behind the collaboration was to provide an imagined soundtrack to F.W. Murnau's 1922 silent horror film of the same name, and the record was dedicated to the actor Max Schreck, who played its vampiric main character, the spectral Count Orlok.

Vampires are of course interstitial creatures, existing on the boundary between life and death, and *Nosferatu* was writhing in demonology and grotesque anthropomorphisms. The inner sleeve featured a picture of a Japanese Hannya mask, which represents a female demon in Noh theatre, while songs such as "Big Bug" (about Leon Trotsky's armoured train), "Irate Caterpillar" (about the avant-garde guitarist Fred Frith) and "Puppets" (denouncing the manipulations of the music industry) populated the claustrophobic soundscape with a menagerie of the bizarre. "Wrong Way Round", which featured the circus calls of Ian Dury, described a girl who had been built, impossibly, back to front. "Mothra" was perhaps the most suggestive track on the album, recalling as it did not only the Japanese pulp monster after which it was named, but also *The Mothman Prophecies*, a book by the UFO researcher John Keel, which had been published four years earlier.

Keel was an associate of The Stranglers who would occasionally hook up with the band during their American tours. *The Mothman Prophecies* was notable in that like the French researcher Jacques Vallée's *Passport To Magonia*, and indeed Ted Holiday's *The Goblin Universe*, it rejected the idea that UFOs were the transports of alien visitors from Outer Space (the so-called "extraterrestrial hypothesis") and instead examined the UFO phenomenon from a cultural perspective, locating it within the realm of the bizarre creatures of folklore and the imagination, hallucinatory experience, and the phenomena of the paranormal. During his researches into the fabled "Mothman", a winged humanoid who had terrified witnesses prior to the collapse of the Silver Bridge at Point Pleasant, West Virginia in 1967, Keel had noted how Meninblack reports had often followed in the wake of these events, and had posited the phenomenon as being part of a kind of cosmic counter-intelligence operation; a means by which whatever "intelligence" lay behind these disparate anti-structural activities tried to point responsibility back towards the equally impenetrable realm of human bureaucratic institutions. They were The Trickster's means of covering his trail.

In the meantime, the aura of misfortune continued to close in on The Stranglers. On returning from their Japanese tour in mid-December, they discovered that the cheque from the promoter had been deliberately written in sterling rather than yen, rendering it unredeemable. On Christmas day Kevin Sparrow, the designer of the band's logo and the *Black And White* album sleeve, died after drinking a combination of tranquilisers and whisky.

At his court hearing in the New Year, Cornwell was sentenced to two months in prison, which was considered a particularly harsh sentence for a first offence. The judge made it clear that the Stranglers frontman was being made an example of. Later that month the "Bear Cage" single was released. This song was overtly about imprisonment, in this instance the giant open-air prison that was West Berlin. Not only did that city have a bear on its coat of arms, but it was also being kept in captivity by a bear – the Russian one. There were hopes at this time that Cornwell would win his appeal and be spared gaol, but the promotional video that accompanied the record betrays the group's pessimism. It plays like a surreal nightmare, in which the fighter pilot Cornwell is shot down in his Spitfire, and falls to Earth, only to be dragged into a holiday-cum-prison-camp, named "Bearlins," by club-wielding redcoats, who were portrayed by the other members of the band.

On the 21st March, the appeal was held at Knightsbridge Crown Court. The omens were good, as Paul Loasby on his appeal had had his sentence replaced by a fine. Cornwell's lawyer put on a thoroughly convincing bravura performance in front of the panel of three judges, likening the amount of heroin that was in the singer's possession to a single sniff from a snuff tin. The panel then retired to deliberate, returning five minutes later to uphold the sentence. Cornwell was immediately taken down to the holding cells to await transportation to Pentonville prison.

Orpheus had entered the underworld, and though Pentonville wasn't the toughest prison in London, it was one of the oldest and filthiest, crawling as it was with rats and cockroaches. Cornwell's account of his stay in prison, "Inside Information", which he narrated to the Record Mirror journalist Barry Cain on his release, alternates between poignant vignettes of the hopeless fates of many of his fellow inmates, and diatribes against the bureaucracy of the prison system, which seemed to have been purposely designed to create as much misery and frustration as possible. The requirement to fill in forms for the most elementary of concessions, and then submit them within almost impossibly narrow time limits, was particularly disturbing to an individual whose very being had been predicated on flouting rules, but the purpose of this seemingly pointless bureaucracy was to instill the lesson that authority dictates structure, and structure dictates hierarchy. That this "rational" structure appeared irrational to the inmates was irrelevant; it served a definite purpose for those who had devised it. Yet it also provided a model of how the disenchantment of the world had, as one of its inherent traits, the tendency to foster uncertainty and alienation. Bureaucracy is by its nature opaque and contradictory, subject to what Ivan Illich called "irrational consistency", and here, within the greyest, deadest, most perfect expression of rationalism, anti-structure could fester.

Cornwell's incarceration had necessarily affected the rest of the group. The Stranglers had been scheduled to be the first Western band to play in India, but the tour had had to be cancelled, the honour instead going, inevitably, to The Police. It is one of the stranger ironies of the band's history that the chief beneficiaries of their misfortune happened to be named after the primary enforcers of state authority. The band had also scheduled two dates at the Rainbow theatre on the Easter weekend of April the 3rd and 4th to showcase new material. In the event more established songs were chosen, with the vocals provided by the group's friends and labelmates; the performers including Ian Dury, Toyah Wilcox, Steel Pulse, Richard Jobson, Jake Burns, The Cure and Cornwell's then-girlfriend Hazel O'Connor. Though the concerts were promoted as benefit gigs for Cornwell, it is significant that none of the really high-status figures within the punk movement felt the necessity to demonstrate their support.

Ultimately, the Rainbow gigs underlined The Stranglers' artificially low status.

Prisoner F48444 was released from Pentonville on 25th April 1980 after serving five weeks of his eight-week sentence for good behaviour. A month later the "Who Wants The World?" single was released, this having been recorded at The Church studio during March, just before Cornwell lost his appeal. It was the first single overtly based around the Meninblack concept, and was a re-statement of the band's gnosticism. In this case an alien visitor arrives on Earth to see how the humans that have been planted there have ruined it through their rapacity. The rhetorical question of the song's title is plaintively answered by Cornwell: *"Not me, not me."*

The alien leaves to see the *"setting sunrise"* of nuclear war; the inevitable destiny of mankind's corruption. The B-side, "The Meninblack (Waiting For 'Em)" was a chilling instrumental built around an ominous, hypnotic drum-pattern, and was intended as a preview of the group's new material. In contrast to their previous work, this was to be meticulously recorded under the total control of The Stranglers themselves. Demonstrating the measured, bridge-building diplomacy that had come to characterize the band, Cornwell had told the NME in November 1979:

We're never going to use a producer again. They are just shitty little parasites. All they're good for is telling jokes. And we know better jokes than any of 'em.

The sessions for the band's fifth album, "The Gospel According To The Meninblack", were to be conducted in complete contrast to the urgent, intimate and inexpensive methodology that had been adopted under Martin Rushent. The band were to spend months ranging across Europe and the UK in order to use the most expensive and well-equipped studios available, and would adopt a number of increasingly bizarre techniques in order to disrupt the organic flow of their music.

The recordings were to begin in the disco producer Giorgio Moroder's Musicland studios, that were buried in a basement under the drab 23-storey Arabella Hochhaus hotel in Munich. Queen had just completed recording their disco-themed *The Game* album before The Stranglers had moved in, and the dank, oppressive atmosphere of Musicland had deeply disturbed Freddie Mercury, causing him to flee the studio at every available opportunity. The experience of the new occupants was to be no happier.

The band brought engineer Steve Churchyard along with them, and he was to witness the bizarre, yet effective, recording technique that Jet Black had evolved on the *The Raven*. The drummer played each component of his kit separately, starting with just the kick drum on the first track of the tape, then the snare drum on the next track, followed in turn by the hi-hats, cymbals and tom-toms, all on their own discrete tracks. This required superlative timing from Black, but the advantage it gave was that it allowed each part of the kit to be manipulated and treated separately during the mixing stage. The drums were to be further abstracted by an innovation on the part of Cornwell, who had discovered that portable tape recorders contained condenser microphones that compressed sound. The singer had mounted these tape recorders from microphone stands over the drum kit, giving the resulting tracks a metallic sheen. The result was that Black had become a kind of human drum machine, granting the songs on *The Gospel* an uncanny interstitial aura, neither analogue nor digital.

The band had managed to lay down two tracks, "Thrown Away" and "Second Coming", when, one Sunday while Black and Cornwell were working in the studio, a white-coated engineer from the Munich Telephone Company arrived and proceeded to work on a cable rack behind the mixing desk. There was then a spark and a puff of smoke, and the power supply for the Harrison recording console went down. As there were only two of these in Europe at the time, five days were lost while trying to track down a replacement power supply, and the recording fell behind schedule.

The Stranglers decamped to the more familiar surroundings of EMI's Pathe Marconi studios in Paris, staying in a hotel that, according to Burnel, they couldn't afford. By now, the band were referring to themselves as Hughinblack, JJinblack, Daveinblack and Jetinblack, so completely did they identify with the Meninblack concept, even insisting that they be addressed as such during interviews. Just as their music was becoming abstracted, so were the band's personal relationships, each member seeming to exist in a bubble, having his own time schedule and unique interpretation of the Meninblack mythos. As Hugh Cornwell was to tell Jim Drury:

We were all high on different substances, doing interviews in different rooms and saying completely different things. We actually liked the idea of giving conflicting stories at this time because this created controversy.

The different drug habits concomitantly produced divergent sleeping patterns for the various members, and so another engineer, Laurence Diana, arrived in Paris to assist Steve Churchyard, and allow recording to be undertaken around the clock. The band were split into two units, with Churchyard working with Cornwell and Black, and Diana working with Burnel and Greenfield. Cornwell was to liken it to a factory system, with a division of labour between band members and their respective studio rooms, sometimes with three or four members each working on different track in a separate studio simultaneously. The latest technology was employed to thread the disparate tracks together, as Hugh Cornwell was to recall:

The studios we used had these new Solid State Logic recording desks. You could record the settings on different channels for each sound and then save them on computer disk. If you wanted to remix the song you just put in the disk and recalled the settings of all the sounds. If you wanted to keep the drum sound the same, but the keyboard sound slightly different, you could do this easily. It wasn't very organic, but the engineers and producers loved it

Three tracks were completed in Paris, "Waltzinblack", "Four Horsemen", and "Hallow To Our Men", before it was time to switch locations again, to the RCA studios in Rome. During the interim, a short European tour was scheduled to take up the remainder of June and early July, after which recording would recommence. The tour began in France and proceeded normally until the date in Cannes on June 20th was cancelled by the venue owner, reputedly because he had just got wind of The Stranglers' reputation. A replacement gig was urgently arranged for that evening at Nice University.

Unknown to the band themselves they were about to play in an institution in which the students were already harbouring deep political grievances toward the University administrators. The band were made to feel most unwelcome by the liaison committee, and were allocated a power supply that was completely insufficient for the needs of their equipment. They were refused permission to use a hired generator on the implausible grounds that it would melt the concrete. During the concert, the inevitable happened, with the PA system failing on four occasions, each one requiring the group to walk off stage while the road crew attempted to restore the power. After the fourth power failure the group felt they had no option but to abort the gig. Burnel explained to the audience, in French, that the problems weren't The Stranglers' fault, and asked them not to take out their frustrations on the band's equipment. The lights then went out and chaos ensued, with the windows of the glass auditorium being smashed by the furious students. The group gingerly made their way out of the back door of the auditorium, their equipment intact, and left the venue just as three vans full of riot police were arriving.

The band members were arrested as they individually arrived back at their hotel later that evening, and taken to the local prison, the Maison d'Arret de Nice, where they were to remain for 10 days while their manager Ian Grant tried desperately to locate them and persuade a tardy EMI to provide bail funds. After just 57 days at large, Cornwell was back behind bars. The band were paired off into two cells, with Cornwell and Burnel in one, and Black and Greenfield in the other. The cells were extremely primitive, with stone plinths and blankets for bedding, and a hole in the floor serving as a toilet and cockroach access passage.

Greenfield was released early, as, characteristically, he hadn't spoken to the audience that evening, while the others were faced with the possibility of a ten year sentence for inciting a riot, a serious crime in France. In a photograph taken prior to the bail hearing, that appeared on the cover of the later "Nice In Nice" single, Jet Black, always the psychologically strongest member of the group, can be seen raising his fist in defiance. Burnel who is handcuffed to him, holds his fist up with less conviction, while the demoralised Cornwell tries to hide himself from the camera.

The group were bailed for six months and proceeded to Rome, where in the event, little recording was achieved. They then returned to Britain, and completed the remaining tracks of the album during August 1980 at Pebble Beach Sound Studio in Worthing, and Startling Sounds in Tittenhurst Park, Berkshire, which was John Lennon's former home. Their manager Ian Grant quit the following month, pithily concluding:

They were doing heroin, which effectively made them unmanageable. All this stuff about bad luck and the Men In Black – the bad luck was just foolishness. They were a band that was going to take over the world and the reason they didn't is because they fucked it up. I was constantly thwarted and frustrated.

October saw the band cross the Atlantic for an American tour, and by now disaster had become almost predictable. On the 21st of that month, following a gig at the Ritz club in New York, the truck carrying all the band's equipment was stolen, including the instruments that they had worked with for many years. Particularly hard hit was Dave Greenfield, who had customised much of his gear. The band managed to complete the tour using hired equipment, but after they returned home they found that former manager Ian Grant had only paid the first installment of the group's insurance before his departure, leaving them effectively uninsured. This second misfortune would cost them an estimated £46,000.

Also during the tour, The Stranglers' roadie Alan McStravich suffered a heart attack after snorting ketamine while packing up after a gig. He had mistaken the powerful horse tranquiliser for cocaine and was flown home, a physical wreck, shortly afterwards. Later in the year one of the group's tour managers, Charlie Pile, would die of cancer. At the time, the band were convinced that the misfortunes that were striking their friends and associates were related to the Meninblack phenomenon.

There was a chink of light at the end of December, when at the trial in Nice the band were given a year's suspended sentence and a fine of 17,000 Francs. With the cloud of potential prison sentences out of the way, the record company could set about releasing The Stranglers' new material, though EMI's efforts at promoting this curious band they had inherited from United Artists was rarely enthusiastic.

The first single from the forthcoming LP, "Thrown Away" was released on the 19th January 1981, and went where all Stranglers 7-inchers now went – to the outer fringes of the Top 40. Lyrically it was a restatement of the sentiments expressed in "Who Wants

The World?" with an alien visitor once more voicing disappointment at mankind's carelessness in ruining the world that the extra-terrestrials had especially created for him. The punishment would be the seeding of religion:

Our ships will stay for just a moment
Leaving false Gods and hypocrisy

The Gospel According To The Meninblack album was released on the 7th of February, to critical disdain and general public befuddlement. Though often erroneously described as a concept album, it actually wasn't, as it didn't feature the central narrative arc of the archetypal prog-rock concept. It would be more accurate to call it a group of songs clustered around a narrow central theme, though this again wouldn't be quite correct, as although it might have appeared that way viewing it from the outside, from The Stranglers' own perspective it heterogeneously explored the entirety of their worldview. That the record went straight into the album charts at Number 8 showed that expectations of the group were still fairly high, but the record would disappear from the charts only five weeks later.

On a first listen, the record appears impenetrable and uninviting, having a hard technological edge without any accompanying sheen or smoothness. This is because the method of composition and recording, taking analogue instruments and sounds and then synthesizing them in the mixing process, locates the songs in an unfamiliar liminal realm between the organic and the technological. The revelation of its baroque patterning and exquisite textures required a perseverance that few listeners were prepared to undertake.

The opening piece, "Waltzinblack" was a dance macabre, a tarantula of a track, in which the juddering waltz-time rhythm welcomes the unholy host of the Meninblack, whose mocking laughter builds until it echoes across the cosmos. There is a sense in which they are not only ridiculing the listener, but also their creators, The Stranglers themselves. For what was intriguing in the misfortunes that plagued the band during this period is that whatever *thing* was directing them, it seemed to have the intention of preventing them from creating this very record. The incarcerations, the studios blowing up, the recording sessions disrupted, the instruments stolen; they all conformed to a pattern whose ulterior motive seemed to be to prevent the band exploring the Meninblack phenomenon any further, even if that meant destroying their career. And now, on the release of the record that was meant to bring the Meninblack to public attention, the group had a commercial disaster on their hands.

In fact, disruption is a commonplace for investigators of UFOs and other paranormal phenomena. John Keel himself was the victim of numerous bizarre telephone pranks while he was investigating the "mothman" case. It is an axiom of anti-structure that it does not like to be probed or brought to attention; its arena is the marginal, and it is in the margins that it prefers to remain. Whether the Trickster is a supernatural entity "out there", or whether he is merely a product of the individual or collective unconscious is a particularly vexed question when it comes to The Stranglers, as their conception of the Meninblack was plainly at least partly an abstraction of themselves, and they had proved adept at self-sabotage even before the creation of their alien alter-egos. The answer, implicity, can never be known.

The second song on the album, "Just Like Nothing On Earth", begins with the descending sound of an alien spaceship landing on Earth. In fact, according to JJinblack, the sound is of four separate craft, each carrying a member of the band. Daveinblack's opening synthesizer riff replicates a didgeridoo, the Australian aboriginal communication instrument, and this is fitting, as the creation myth of the indigenous tribes of Australia was particularly suggestive of the alien astronaut concept of the Meninblack, evoking as it did a race of heroes who, during the timeless era of "The Dreaming" created sacred sites on a previously formless landscape.

Hughinblack's guitar riff was based on the "high-life" style of Zaire, whereas the tongue-twisting lyrics summarised a number of bizarre stories he had read in UFO periodicals, including a woman in New Zealand who claimed to have been abducted by aliens and forced to have sex with them in their spacecraft, and a Japanese man who had awoken in his car only to find an alien sitting next to him.

Stories of alien abduction would reach epidemic proportions during the late 1980s and 1990s, in which "victims" were taken aboard spaceships, placed on floating tables, and subjected to various forms of degrading examination, such as being sexually molested, impregnated with alien children, or having their bodily organs extracted and replaced. Many of these events would be recalled under hypnosis, when the individual concerned was receiving psychological treatment for quite different reasons. However, as John Michael Greer pointed out in his book *The UFO Phenomenon*, the template for alien abduction may have far deeper psychological and cultural roots than is acknowledged by believers in the extra-terrestrial origin of UFOs. He noted that shamanic rites involved being accompanied to other realms by humanoid, but non-human, figures:

Siberian shamans in their initiatory trances experience having their organs removed and replaced with new, magical organs, just as abductees undergo baroque medical procedures and experience having implants placed in their bodies. Just as visionaries around the world have claimed that they receive spiritual gifts from their experiences, too, a sizeable number of abductees believe that they have gained psychic powers in the aftermath of their abductions.

Greer also examined the work of Dr. Alex Krul and Ken Phillips, on the backgrounds of UFO witnesses, and observed:

Compared to control groups, people who report a close encounter with a UFO are significantly more likely to be dissatisfied with their lives, to have problems with nervousness, to recall their dreams, to have had flying dreams or dreams about UFO's, and to report experience of ESP ... these may seem like a grab-bag of unrelated psychological traits, but they are nothing of the kind. In cultures around the world, these are recognised as among the hallmarks of a potential shaman.

These traits also conform to Ernest Hartmann's mind theory of "thin boundaries", and Hartmann also linked such thin mental boundaries not only to hypnosis, synesthesia, lucid dreaming, and paranormal experiences, but also, crucially, to a low social status. In a rationalised, disenchanted world, in which status is linked to acceptance of the prevailing materialist dogma, the shamanic experience, which may be intrinsic to the human condition, becomes nothing more than a "superstitious" hangover, discounted by high-status science and academia and experienced only by the socially marginal.

"Second Coming" posited the return of Jesus to Earth, and his subsequent rejection. The song was inspired by Hughinblack's time in Pentonville, where he requested a Bible with the intention of turning it into a pack of playing cards, but which he subsequently ended up reading. As he was to state in *Song By Song*:

We always thought the ideas of the Meninblack, UFO's and religion went hand in hand. There are a lot of references in The Bible to visions appearing in the sky, to seraphims and burning chariots. If you were a peasant living in time BC, a chariot was a form of transport, but a burning chariot could have been a spaceship or flying saucer. Someone in biblical times might say 'I saw something go over my head. It was moving, it had a flame and I saw a man in it. Therefore it's a burning chariot with an angel inside.' UFO

experts have always recognised that the visions seen by people in the
Bible could be interpreted as alien visitations.

Of course, the opposite could also be true: the alien visitations
witnessed during the late twentieth century could be interpreted
as contemporary Biblical visions. One of the first observers to
note the mythical dimension of the UFO phenomenon was the
Swiss psychologist Carl Jung. In his 1958 book *Flying Saucers: A*
Modern Myth of Things Seen in the Skies, Jung noted how a generation raised on science rather than spirituality could no longer
believe in the old archetypes of angels and devils, and so had
dressed them up in the technological raiments of rockets and
spaceships. The threat of nuclear destruction had created a
feverish millenarianism, and as the Messiah could no longer be
faithfully expected, so the Flying Saucers had arrived instead.

John Michael Greer posited that the arrival of the UFOs had an
antecedent in The Great Chain Of Being. This was the doctrine,
universal in the Western world during the Middle Ages and
Rennaissance and still common until the late nineteenth century,
that the cosmos was alive with intelligent entities, from God
downwards to the humblest of rocks, of which humans formed
the middle link. This Great Chain cascaded downwards from
humanity through the apes and lower mammals to the simplest
living organisms and inert matter. But it also spiralled upwards
through various disembodied spirits, angels and archangels to
the Lord himself. The Enlightenment, and the scientific
revolution, with its mechanical philosophy, tended to occlude the
upper half of The Great Chain, as its very ineffability made it
unbecoming to scientific examination, and therefore merely
"superstition", whereas the lower half of the chain was
strengthened by the theories of evolution and natural selection,
which emphasized the similarities between all living physical
things. However, this archetypal idea of the universe being
inhabited by higher "intelligences" was recapitulated in the

degraded contemporary notion of extra-terrestrial beings who were more advanced in the purely technological sense.

The gatefold inner sleeve to *The Gospel* featured a corruption of da Vinci's "The Last Supper", in which a Maninblack can be seen in the place of Philip the Apostle. The Meninblack had given birth to religion, and their own second coming was expected on the next track, "Waiting For The Meninblack", the instrumental version of which had been released as a teaser on the B-side of "Who Wants The World?"

"Waiting For The Meninblack" is an intensely sinister piece of music, perfectly suited to the paranoid concept of the Men In Black, whose job it is to ward off scrutiny of UFO sightings and other paranormal events. It is notable, and no accident, that their usually ascribed attire of black suit, black trilby, narrow tie and sunglasses is also the standard dress of United States' Government agents, especially those of the secretive FBI and CIA. George Hansen has noted how the secret services are prodigious manufacturers of paranoia through their usage of deception, which is an innate quality of the Trickster, and he has described how the CIA became almost totally paralysed by the fear that their KGB adversaries were using the same counterintelligence techniques against them as they themselves were using against the Russians. Once deception is engaged in it has a corrosive effect, as the consequent introduction of ambiguity in any social relationship is inherently unbounded.

Paranoia is also closely related to the paranormal, and it is significant that the only rationalised bureaucratic institutions who have engaged in paranormal research are military organisations and the intelligence services. In the United States, the CIA, DIA (Defense Intelligence Agency), US Navy and US Army are all known to have conducted research into various aspects of extra-sensory perception (ESP), including mind control and remote viewing. Telepathy is inherently anti-structural as it erases the boundary between self and other, perhaps the most crucial binary in Western rationalism. It introduces the notion that our thoughts are not our own; that they are being generated by others who may not share our best interests. The knowledge that secretive government agencies are experimenting in paranormal activity is bound to generate widespread paranoia, regardless of the intention behind the experiments, or even whether they are efficacious.

US Government agencies were also involved in duplicity regarding the UFO phenomenon in a direct sense. Both Greer and Hansen have identified the US Air Force's Office of Special Investigations (AFOSI) as having deliberately seeded journalists with stories of alien bases on Earth, and alien involvement in cattle mutilations. Greer has noted how many of the UFO enthusiast and witness groups were infiltrated by government operatives. The most respected organisation, the National Investigation Committee on Aerial Phenomena (NICAP) was heaving with CIA and Air Force assets, including board members Admiral Roscoe Hillenkoetter, Karl Pflock, Colonel Joseph J. Bryan III, and Nicholas de Rochefort. The latter two were, incidentally, the head of the CIA's psychological warfare department, and his assistant. Similarly, the head of the Center for UFO Studies (CUFOS), the influential J. Allen Hynek, was also connected to the intelligence services through the Air Force's Foreign Technology Division.

On the sceptical side of the UFO controversy, many of the debunkers of the Committee for Scientific Investigation of Claims of the Paranormal (CSICOP) also had connections to the intelligence services, including Donald Menzel, a former codebreaker who had worked as a contractor for the CIA and National Security Agency (NSA), and Philip Klass who routinely disseminated Air Force disinformation through his *Aviation Week* magazine. The important result was that any mysterious sighting, whether it was hailed as proof of alien visitors, or debunked as merely a sighting of Venus through a heat haze, was never identified as what it probably was: a secret military aircraft flying out of Lockheed Martin's Skunk Works.

If the UFO phenomenon was partly a revivification of atavistic human visionary capabilities, it was also mainly a US Government deception programme to bury sightings of proto-types of advanced aircraft in a haze of misinformation. This deception came at a price though; it introduced paranoia into the culture at large, and eroded trust in the US Government and its machinery. And what of the Men In Black? Initially they may have been real government agents warding witnesses away from genuinely classified hardware. However, their cultural presence is best explained by the concept of projection, which George Hansen describes as an intrinsic element of paranoia. In traditional non-Western societies where the boundaries of subject and object are not so discretely separated and delineated, the projection of intra-group or intra-tribal conflicts onto external entities, whether real or imaginary, is a commonplace. The anthropologist Henry Sharp described how a conflict between two brothers in a Chipewyan society was sublimated by a hunt for the mythical Bigfoot. Similarly, misfortunes, illnesses and death within indigenous tribes the world over are explained by the presence of witches and sorcerers. In contemporary Western society, the boundary-thinning or -erasing effects of paranoia may invoke a similar projection mechanism, with totem figures of the inscrutable, unfathomable bureaucracy invoked as its target. The Men In Black may be projected "Government Men", an overt visualisation of the mysterious agency of the State.

Such a projection would have been attractive to the marginalised Stranglers, who occupied a low status even by the outcast standards of punk. But it is important not to go too far; the anti-structural nature of the Men In Black phenomenon means that it can never be fully explained, and there may be elements to it that cannot be understood by any "rational" formulation.

"Turn, The Centuries, Turn" was a Black Iron Prison of an

instrumental that had the density of an imploding star. Its centre-piece was a sicky-yellow backwards guitar solo that sounded like time unwinding into the void. "Four Horsemen", sung by Daveinblack, was one of the very finest pieces of music that The Stranglers composed, built around a shifting time structure in which, during designated sections, beats were either added to, or subtracted from, each consecutive bar. The lyrics were once more inspired by Nostradamus, and imagined the Four Horsemen of the Apocalypse arriving on Earth in spaceships rather than on horseback. There was also the possibility that the Four Horsemen were The Stranglers themselves.

"Manna Machine" was inspired by the book of the same name by George Sassoon and Rodney Dale, which like other "ancient astronaut" theories such as Berger and Pauwel's *Morning of the Magicians*, and Erich Von Däniken's *Chariots Of The Gods?*, posited a technological basis for early historic sacred structures and religious myths. The book alleged that the machine created manna, a kind of edible frost or dew, by purifying the air. It was powered by the Ark of the Covenant, which was a small nuclear reactor, and was given to the Israelites by a race of aliens to sustain them during their 40-year period of wandering in the Sinai, the secrets of its operation being coded into the Jewish Kabbalah.

The ominous throb was created from a drum loop made by Jetinblack that was too long to fit on a tape deck, and so was threaded around pencils held by the individual band members in different points in the studio. This alien pulse not only evokes the buried but still-operative manna machine, but also an Egyptian mummy, suggesting that the machine, like a dead Pharaoh, may be best left undisturbed.

The Israelites' 40 years of wandering was also evoked in the final song on the album, "Hallow To Our Men", in which Hughinblack pleads with the Meninblack to provide the sterile Earth with manna. The Israelites were punished with their wanderings when, after they were freed from the bondage of Pharaoh, they refused to enter the Promised Land of Canaan. Corrupted by the cities of the Egyptians, their faith in the promises of Yahweh was equivocal, and so they suffered. For The Stranglers, Yahweh was a mythologised interpretation of alien Gods who were inherently ambiguous and capricious. "Hallow To Our Men" exalts them, but with a halting sense of trepidation. When their craft can be heard ascending again at the very end of the record, there is a palpable sense of relief.

And so there should have been, as with their departure the Meninblack saga was over, and the band's traumas and tribulations were, as if by magic, to come to an end. As Cornwell was to tell Jim Drury:

> We'd got so used to things going wrong that we couldn't see a link. It was only when we stopped with the Meninblack and the light started shining again and we realised there had been a change. After we had purged ourselves of our Meninblack obsession, we moved on ... how much of what happened was coincidental and how much was caused by ourselves, I don't know.

The Stranglers' career had unravelled with remarkable rapidity. The release of *The Raven* in September 1979 had been accompanied with supreme optimism on the part of the band's management and record company. By March 1981, a mere 18 months later, the group, abandoned by almost everyone who had ever shown faith in them, and critically derided more than they had ever been before, faced ruin. As with Cornwell, Jean Jacques Burnel was to identify the adoption of heroin as a key turning point:

> I'm convinced that when you do things like smack, you enter a different world. People who are down on themselves or who think the world is black tend to be unlucky people. We were in this terrible

situation, although we didn't see it as terrible at the time. Unlucky, bad, negative things would happen to us. And then we all stopped – well, sort of. You don't just stop doing heroin ... (t)he sound of the Meninblack album was definitely a product of our drugged state of mind. We were bankrupt by the end of the album.

The Gospel According To The Meninblack was the band's most inscrutable record, and yet also their masterpiece, and such a paradox is entirely fitting. The Stranglers had entered an interstitial realm, and tried to make sense of it from the inside, but the essence of anti-structure is that it is the breakdown of Western logical thought and categorisation, and a return to what Lucien Lévy-Bruhl called "pre-logical" thinking, in which the hard binaries that constitute our classification systems no longer apply. In their place is something more akin to the totemic categorisations of "primitive" peoples, in which sympathetic links thread together the most unlikely beings and objects, and the boundary between self and other is no longer so distinct. The Stranglers were no longer dissociated from their environment by the distancing effects of Western rationalism. Planet Earth was a prison that only brought misfortune. The basement of Musicland studios was a prison that only brought misfortune. Pentonville was a prison that only brought misfortune. New associations had been formed that were "logically" impossible, but, nevertheless, powerfully efficacious. As Hugh Cornwell was to relate:

The thing that hit me hardest occurred when I was taken to Pentonville immediately after the appeal. The guards took all my clothes away from me and gave me a uniform that didn't fit. This really dented my confidence. It was suddenly brought home to me that I was being stripped of my identity. I'll never forget that moment. Everything else paled into insignificance to the effect that had on me. It rocked my whole existence.

What Cornwell had experienced here was the devastating lowering of status that is the result of entanglement in the Trickster constellation, and this experience was far from unique to The Stranglers. George Hansen documents numerous episodes in which small, self-reinforcing groups became immersed in occult beliefs, often involving UFOs, with spectacularly destructive results. Perhaps the most bizarre case involved Psi Tech, a private company that was spun off from the CIA's remote viewing programme to advise commercial businesses. After a promising start, it suddenly started to make preposterous claims that the Earth was receiving visits from angelic superbeings, that it could locate Mozart's grave, and that a nest of pregnant extraterrestrial hybrid women would emerge from a cavern in New Mexico in the summer of 1993. Its founder members, many of them high-ranking officers in the US Army, went on to suffer marital breakdowns and even in one case a psychotic episode that resulted in hospitalisation. Exposure to the paranormal, and its inherently anti-structural properties, can have a ruinous effect even on the most disciplined individuals.

For The Stranglers, the long, slow climb back towards daylight began in July 1981, with the writing of material for the *La Folie* album. In contrast to the baroque recording methodology adopted for *The Gospel According To The Meninblack*, the new record was to be a back-to-basics affair. The band attempted to replicate the atmosphere of the early days in Guildford and Chiddingford by writing and rehearsing as an ensemble at Jet Black's house in Gloucestershire, and then moving straight to Virgin Records' Manor Studios the following month to lay down the recording.

La Folie, released in November 1981, was very much viewed as The Stranglers' last chance by their record company, EMI, and the first single from the LP, "Let Me Introduce You To The Family" followed the disappointing pattern of barely breaking the Top 40 that had been inaugurated by "Nuclear Device" two years earlier. Worse, the album itself was the first by the group that failed to make the Top 10 on its first week of release. The record itself took its title from the French term for "Madness", and was loosely conceptual, with each song purporting to examine a different aspect of love. The record also contained the last glowing embers of the band's anti-structuralism, containing as it did their final allusions to narcotics, murder and cannibalism.

Ironically, it would be one of these embers that would provide the lifeline that the band were desperately seeking. "Golden Brown" emerged from a piece of music that Dave Greenfield had originally composed as a sequential part of "Second Coming" from the *Meninblack* album. Cornwell, on hearing it in isolation, was inspired to write accompanying lyrics, and present it to the rest of the band. The song was the consummation of the theme that he had cultivated with "Toiler On The Sea" and "Baroque Bordello"; the boundary-blurring conflation of erotic love and pharmacopia as a recreation of the timeless bliss of the womb, with a ship once more employed as the protective metaphor.

When it was released as the second single from *La Folie* in April 1982, there was little faith in it either from the band or the record company, with only Jet Black having any expectations of success. Although it is now by far the most famous Stranglers song, and has perhaps become over-familiar as the signature song of the group, it is easy to forget just what a curious, uncanny song it was on its release, so divorced was it from the eager bustle of the usual chart fare. It sounded like it had arrived from a different dimension, one where time no longer applied; its stillness magically suspended the movement of the everyday world. It also contained an intriguing metaphor of addiction as bondage:

Every time just like the last
On her ship tied to the mast

Again we see the bizarre interrelationship between the deliberate choice by the band to take heroin, and their subsequent incarceration, though an awareness of this was there from the start, in the ball-and-chain chords of "Don't Bring Harry". Heroin was the drug that both imprisoned Cornwell in addiction, and literally landed him in prison. Perhaps, oddly, "Golden Brown" may be the most extreme expression of The Stranglers' worldview, suggesting that the only escape from the world-as-prison is to the eternal, ecstatic incarceration of the womb; the gateway between the two worlds being provided by opium.

Even beyond the subject matter of the lyrics, "Golden Brown" had a most unlikely structure for a hit single, being arranged in the compound waltz time signature of 13/8, in the key of B flat minor, with the melody being played on that antiquated instrument the harpsichord. Remarkably, it reached Number 2 in the charts and stayed there for a fortnight. Proving that The Trickster hadn't quite finished with the band yet, the song was prevented from reaching the top spot by a combination of the retro-novelty act Tight Fit and EMI's failure to press enough copies to meet demand. After this event, Jet Black was to refer to the company as Every Mistake Imaginable.

"Golden Brown" had salvaged The Stranglers' career, and, distrusting EMI, the group took advantage of a loophole in their contract to sign with CBS records, who had promised them complete artistic freedom. As part of the severance deal, The Stranglers left EMI with a new recording of "Strange Little Girl", a demo of which the label had rejected back in 1975. "Strange Little Girl", which was a Top Ten hit that July, was another ineffably haunting song, its perversity lying in the fact that it was about the same girl as the violent "Sometimes" from the debut album, and also that, for once, there were no hidden meanings. Any darkness ascribed to the song came purely from the listener.

A few months earlier, during March 1982, BBC West had aired

a documentary made by Cornwell and Black, called, appropriately, "The Colour Black", which was, in effect, their final
farewell to the Meninblack concept. The programme was a giddy
mixture of the quaint and the sinister, in which the intrepid pair
examined how black, an "absence of colour", pervaded the
power structures of authority, from religious leaders, to the
police, to the judiciary. They noted also that black was the colour
of oil and coal, the energy sources that provided a different kind
of power to the rulers of the West. But was this accidental? Or
was there some kind of cosmic design behind it? After numerous
vox pops, and interviews with a professor and a vicar, the
programme ended with the two Stranglers, dressed in
Meninblack suits, driving a black Cadillac to an isolated
farmhouse out in the yonder.

On the first day of 1983, The Stranglers released their last truly
great album, *Feline*. It was another radical departure musically,
being performed on the unusual instrumental combination of
synthesizers, drum machines, and acoustic guitars, the former
two symbolising the industrial north of Europe, and the latter the
agricultural south. *Feline* was probably the most coherent
Stranglers long player since *Rattus Norvegicus*, though it provided
a marked counterpoint to that debut record. Like *Rattus* it was
thematically entirely nocturnal and urban, but whereas the first
album throbbed with seamy, scarlet life, the city of *Feline* was
cold and deserted. The cat had eaten the rat. The tone was
valedictory; the last wine flowed as the restaurants emptied.

We're away
Every day

London, Paris, Rome, New York, were ruins. Like the Venice of
Nicholas Roeg's "Don't Look Now", the streets and alleys of
Feline were mysterious, shadowy and abandoned. They had been
abandoned by The Stranglers' alien muses, the Meninblack, and

Cornwell and Burnel were now diminished figures, searching hopelessly amongst the beautiful latinates and arabesques of sound they had constructed for their extraterrestrial alter egos.

Black friend of the night
Why did you leave in such a hurry?

The great beast was dead, and *Feline* was its bewitching fossil, the structural relic left behind after the band's colossal, terrifying anti-structuralism had petrified. The exquisite, lifeless production made it sound like it had been recorded in a catacomb. It was a mausoleum, but an endlessly mysterious one, its byzantine passages and chambers marked with the hieroglyphics of a long dead alien race.

There then followed a long recording hiatus of nearly two years during which The Stranglers reorganised themselves into a more consistant, professional unit, and the fundamental means by which this was undertaken was by introducing a more pronounced hierarchical structure to their line-up. Cornwell became more of a traditional front man, taking on almost all of the singing and songwriting. Burnel's role was relegated from a joint, though slightly lesser, frontman to that of a more traditional sideman. Greenfield, who had once been the sole source of musical embellishment, found himself increasingly having to share that role with a brass section, while Jet Black demoted himself to a drum machine programmer, at least during recording sessions.

Both Burnel and Cornwell would wean themselves off heroin, and indeed Cornwell would be clean of all drugs by the end of 1984. The group would no longer unnecessarily court trouble, or be a burden on either their record company or their management. Classy, well-written singles such as "Skin Deep", "Nice In Nice" and "Always The Sun" would still glower like the old days, but their modest chart placings betrayed the fact that the public had lost interest in the band. The accompanying albums studiously avoided controversy. There was even, horror of horrors, a belated attempt to break America.

The outcome of this submission to the dictates of the mainstream was that instead of the band projecting their conflicts outwards, they were, inevitably, projected inwards. The price that Cornwell paid for his elevated status within the group was that he was now the authority figure whom the other members could kick against. During the recording of the song "Souls" for the *Aural Sculpture* LP, Cornwell found a mixtape he and Black had completed stuffed in an envelope with the words *"THIS IS SHIT"* written on it, the culprits being Burnel and Greenfield. Following a backstage disagreement over Burnel's stage performance in Rome in 1985, the bass player kicked Cornwell through a plaster wall. After Cornwell had storyboarded and meticulously edited the video for "Always The Sun", the other band members once again endowed it with the epithet of "shit".

However, the band's discomfort with their own conformism did have another, more creative, outlet, and this was in a series of recordings they made under the pseudonym of *The Upper Volga Corngrowers Co-operative Association Choral Dance Troop Ensemble*. Appearing on the B-sides of the group's 12" singles, and set in a faux-Russian folk idiom, the tales of Vladimir Andropyournosin, a Soviet sub-nucleonic particle physicist, and his bizarre semi-accidental sexual and narcotic adventures, were an allegory of the career of The Stranglers themselves.

After unknowingly eating hallucinogenic bread mould in "Vladimir And Olga", he displeases the Soviet authorities by having an affair with a sailor in "Vladimir And Sergei", then with a camel on the Afghan frontline in "Vladimir And The Beast", and finally with a coke-snorting Cuban male prostitute in "Vladimir Goes To Havana". He finally escapes to Mexico, where he can gaze longingly at the promised land of the USA.

Although accentuated for comic effect, the Vladimir stories, based as they are on an essentially conformist scientist who is directed off the conventional path by drugs, and then immersed in wildly anti-structural behaviour that attracts the punishment of the authorities, offer a clear parallel of the experience of former biochemist Hugh Cornwell, as does the last wistful look at an America that can never quite be reached. Vladimir is constantly being kidnapped by the Soviet state in order to be *"re-integrated and normalised"*, but, though diminished each time, he never quite conforms.

And so it was with The Stranglers. Their attempts to re-integrate and normalise themselves, to be archetypally "ambitious" careerists, were always bound to fail. Cornwell himself didn't recognise this, nor why his attempts to instill a sense of purpose and direction, and of leadership, were resented. A measure of the dark, anti-structural currents that once animated the group is gained by the knowledge that since Hugh Cornwell left the band in 1990, he and the other members have not once directly spoken.

Part II

I Feel Like A Wog

"All forms of violence are a quest for identity. When you live out on the frontier, you have no identity; you're a nobody. Therefore you get very tough. You have to prove you are a somebody, so you become very violent. And so identity is always accompanied by violence. Ordinary people find the need for violence as they lose their identities, and so it's only the threat to peoples' identities that makes them violent. Terrorists, hijackers, these are people minus identity. They are determined to make it somehow, to get coverage, to get noticed."
– Marshall McLuhan, interviewed by Canadian television

"Do you know the song 'A Boy Called Sue'? Being called Jean-Jacques was a bit like that. My mum might as well have called me Sue."
– JJ Burnel, interview with The Independent

* * *

In 1981, the record label Decca released a compilation album of minor punk bands named *Strength Thru Oi!* It was a record that aroused controversy not only for its title, a pun on the Nazi slogan "Strength Through Joy", which its compiler, Socialist Workers Party activist Garry Bushell, implausibly claimed to be unaware of, but also because of its cover star, the skinhead icon Nicky Crane.

Crane was a member of the neo-Nazi British Movement, and had been an instrumental figure in that organisation's violent attacks against Leftists, homosexuals and ethnic minorities. By the time of the record's release he had been convicted and jailed for four years for his role in an attack the previous year on a group of black youths arriving on a train at Woolwich Arsenal railway station. This was merely the latest in a string of violent incidents, including an assault on a West Indian family, and the attempted disruption of an anti-racist concert being held at Jubilee Gardens.

However, unbeknown to his far-right colleagues, Crane was living a double life as a homosexual, frequenting gay pubs and clubs and even appearing in amateur gay pornographic films. Also, he was himself from an immigrant background, his real name being Nicola Vincenzio. He too might as well have been called Sue.

Crane eventually confessed all to Channel 4 television, resulting in the memorably pitiless Sun newspaper byline "Nazi Nick Is A Panzi", before dying from an AIDS-related illness in 1986. The tragic arc of his life had been an almost cartoonishly exaggerated exemplar of one of the foremost crises faced by many of the protagonists of the punk movement; the desperate search to find and maintain an identity. It was this struggle that would be the wellspring of much of the violence of the era, not least that of one of its foremost practitioners, The Stranglers' bassist Jean-Jacques Burnel.

* * *

If the crisis of the Seventies was primarily an economic one, it had the effect of aggravating a number of existing fissures within Britain's national identity, and the identities of individuals within it. Punk, above all else, was an identity crisis writ large, a purgative attempt to bring festering ailments into the open so that at least some kind of resolution could be attempted. There were also elements that transcended parochial concerns – the oil crises that punctured the presumptions of Western hegemony, ever-rising living standards, and the notion of a future of unstoppable technological progress. The USA, which had forcibly wrenched the imperial baton from the United Kingdom, appeared mired in "stagflation", an economic quagmire of combined monetary inflation and stagnant growth. This had been the result of the peaking of America's oil production, thus rendering it import-dependent, and the consequent termination

Strangled

of the convertibility of the US Dollar to gold. The result was a collapse of the post-war Bretton Woods global financial system and a subsequent devaluation of the Dollar.

The post-war years, which had seen the collapse of the British Empire, had revealed a ruling class that appeared ill-equipped to deal with a world in which Britain's diminished stature had led to it being increasingly exposed to economic competition from old rivals and new producers. Outside the periphery of these nations lay the inscrutable menace of the Warsaw Pact, the reach of whose tendrils could only be guessed at. This sense of insecurity manifested itself in tense industrial relations and an accelerating decline in British industry as its manufacturers, no longer sheltered by Imperial Preference, became enmeshed in a vicious circle of deteriorating product quality and dwindling exports.

The jibe levelled by its competitors, that Britain had lost an empire but had not yet found a role, was emphasized by a decline in productivity. No longer in the Director's seat, it was increasingly unable to even provide the furnishings. This crisis in direction in turn provoked a crisis of leadership. A number of attempts by post-war governments to modernise the economy, such as "The White Heat Of Technology" and "The Dash For Growth", had fallen flat. The military and diplomatic humiliations of Suez and Aden had been paralleled by the economic ones of Sterling devaluation and the Three Day Week. There was a sense that the very structure of British society, its embedded patterns of hierarchy and class, was at the very crux of the problem. A new term, "the Establishment" was coined to characterise this impotent elite of Colonel Blimps and Upper Class Twits. The Profumo Affair of the previous decade, in which a minister of state was discovered to be cavorting with call-girls, granted this structure the ineffable stench of decay. Britain, or at least the current incarnation of it, was dying.

This sense of malaise percolated throughout British society, and manifested itself at the level of the individual. The Australian social scientist Alistair Mant, embedded within British industry, noted that what made the industrial relations of the time so resistant to "logical" solutions was that the workers were more suspicious of the kind of people that the management were, rather than what they actually did. For Mant, Britain was a society that had turned its battles inward, rather than outward against its international competitors. As factories and even entire industries folded, the explosion in unemployment that began at the end of the Sixties teetered towards 1 million by the close of the decade; a once inconceivable figure. This not only deprived those unable to find work of an identity-defining role, it created a previously unknown feeling of precariousness among those still employed.

The possibility of finding an identity through a work-role was one of the few compensations that industrial capitalism had granted to those it had uprooted from their traditional agricultural backgrounds and deposited in its factories centuries before. The division of labour may have turned craftsmanship into the mere drudgery of piece-work or assembly, but the sense of being a cog in the machine could at least impart a sense of social necessity. As conditions gradually improved through social pressure from organised workers, a strong sense of individual and collective efficacy could be nurtured.

It was in the traditional male-dominated "breadwinner" roles that the decline in employment was felt most deeply, and this was compounded by the increasing number of women entering the workforce, enhancing that sense of specifically male redundancy. There were other challenges to what had appeared only a couple of decades earlier to be an impregnable social order. In the late Sixties, Roy Jenkins' decriminalisation of homosexuality, legalisation of abortion and relaxation of the divorce laws, all driven by a wave of revulsion at the hypocrisy of the MacMillan era, ushered in the "permissive society". Although these were viewed by the progressively minded as an amelioration of the more repressive aspects of "traditional" British society, they failed to note that in the peculiarly unnatural conditions fostered by industrial capitalism, there were few sympathetic bonds among and between its inhabitants. The morality of the protestant work ethic had erected a rickety scaffolding around social relations that had been eroded by the demands of the machine, and all Harold Wilson's government had done was to pull this scaffolding down to meet the demands of bourgeois convenience.

This sense of anomie would be enhanced by another change that had become more and more visible in the post-war era: the arrival and spread of Commonwealth immigrants from the West Indies, Africa and the Indian sub-continent. This dilution of the comparative homogeneity of British society created some curious reactions. The language of deluge of the Conservative Right soon gave way to the rebirth of the far-Right, in the form of the National Front and the British Movement, who supplanted it with the rhetoric of infection and pollution. The Left responded with the bromides of tolerance and "cultural diversity". In the longer view, however, what was happening to Britain was simply a fairly standard historical process: the influx from the periphery to the centre that is common feature of all dying empires, as those whose lands have been looted follow the trail of their former wealth to where it has been deposited. Rome in AD 400 and Baghdad at the twilight of the Arabian empire were similarly multicultural, and their ethnic diversity similarly conveyed that they were in their twilight years.

The dissolution of identity associated with imperial unwind and capitalist crisis was felt most keenly among two groups: the young, whose identity was still in the process of formation, and those from second generation immigrant backgrounds, who would in any case have been tentatively poised between the cultural assumptions of their parents and those of their adopted home. For both these groups, for whom the struggle to form a coherent identity would be challenging enough in a stable society, the distress was particularly acute. They faced a margin-alised existence of increasingly limited opportunities in education, employment and income. It is no surprise then that as a youth movement, many of punk's leading figures were from immigrant backgrounds, whether Irish (John Lydon, Elvis Costello), Jewish (Keith Levene, Mick Jones), German (Ari Up), Somali (Poly Styrene), Portuguese (Ana Da Silva), Belgian (Siouxsie Sioux) or, in the 2-Tone subculture, West Indian.

It was the attempt to construct a coherent identity, social, sexual, and cultural, that provided the impetus for many of punk's young protagonists. As such, they would utilise any strategy they could, including adopting aliases, clothing themselves in sartorial bricolage, and purloining and profaning cultural symbols. For Jean-Jacques Burnel, perhaps more than any other punk musician, the quest to address his own cultural contradictions and forge an identity within which he could comfortably exist, was the paramount theme of his work. It was not going to be a smooth or attractive process to say the least, but it did eventually achieve some measure of success.

Burnel's earliest attempts to assemble the jigsaw pieces of his origins began at school, where his idiosyncratic political ideas first began to form. He had created a magazine called The Gubernator, and joined the British League Of Youth, an organi-sation that had originally been the youth wing of the Labour Party, but since its official disbandment had maintained an anarchic half-life, becoming a home for rejected ideas from across the political spectrum. These were both to display the character-istic traits of Burnel's subsequent search for identity; the devel-opment of an invulnerable, warrior-like self, and the concurrent construction of a political cause which that self could be dedicated to. These ideas, which would be developed from his early reading of Plato's Republic, and partially shaped by his study of history at both the University of Bradford and Huddersfield Polytechnic, had their wellspring in his ambiguous Anglo-French background, and the subsequent teasing and bullying that would result from it. As he was to tell The Independent:

Overall I just wanted to be English. I'm a British citizen and I sound native, but technically I'm French. Growing up as the kid of French people in those days was tough. There weren't so many immigrants then and I was born in Notting Hill where they all used to come in initially. Being a Frog was not a great option at the time. It got me beaten up on more than one occasion.

Burnel's amalgamation into the embryonic Stranglers had been entirely fortuitous. As a delivery driver for the paint suppliers Brown Brothers, he had given a lift to Gyrth Godwin, who was the singer and lyricist in the band's earliest incarnation, Johnny Sox, who were based at Jet Black's off licence, *The Jackpot*, in Guildford. Cornwell had formed Johnny Sox during his tenure at the University of Lund in Sweden, and had persuaded his bandmates to accompany him on his return to the UK, but, apart from recruiting Black as drummer, they had made little progress, and an argument over lack of commitment would see the original members returning home. Having kept contact with Burnel in the pubs around Guildford, Cornwell happened upon the notion of inviting him to join the embryonic Guildford Stranglers alongside himself and Black.

Burnel, who had trained as a classical guitarist, quickly adopted the bass, and it wasn't long before he and Cornwell had formed a promising writing partnership. This was augmented by the arrival of Hans Wärmling, another former Johnny Sox member who, on Cornwell's invitation, had made a belated trip across the North Sea. The businesses were maintained on a threadbare footing as Burnel and Cornwell interweaved running the off licence in the evening with taking Black's van out in the daytime as perhaps Britain's most unlikely ice-cream men. But any progress the band made musically wasn't being matched by success attracting bookings, and so, in 1975, Wärmling too headed back to Sweden, storming out of the band's means of transport, the ice-cream van, on the way to a Bar Mitzvah in north London. Wärmling was replaced by Dave Greenfield, a Brighton-based keyboard player recruited through the classifieds in Melody Maker, and though it may not have seemed so at the time, the long and painful gestation of the group was nearing completion.

It was this very gestation that was to be the source of one of the chief taunts of the group's detractors, that they were journeymen who had opportunistically jumped on the nascent punk bandwagon, but to Burnel it demonstrated the very contrary; that they were the only truly authentic band in the whole scene. As he was to tell John Robb:

Them [The Clash] and the Pistols were like the Monkees. They were put together by their managers and controlled by their managers and we were quite definitely not ... They were fabricated music, they were exciting of course, there is no question of that but The Stranglers were organic. I mean you would not fabricate a bloke who was 15 years older than the rest of the band, Dave is well, Dave, and Hugh, you can't invent someone like that and also a frog immigrant with a chip on his shoulder – who is a psychopath, educated and plays classical music – you don't fabricate bands like that. You just can't.

Despite their diverse backgrounds, The Stranglers looked oddly apposite together, and were compellingly photogenic. Always dead-eyed and looking right through the observer, they resembled a team of assassins, each of whom specialised in a different means of killing. This strong corporate identity, crystallized in the brash font of the band's logo, provided Burnel with a solid platform from which to he could strengthen his identity. It was his first "sacred cause", the term that the philosopher Eric

Hoffer gave to the salvation ideas that provided a lifeline to the dissolute. In identifying himself entirely with The Stranglers, Burnel ensured that any attack on the group was an attack on him personally, and this was to have baleful consequences on the band's career. As he was to later note:

I think probably politically we fucked it up. We made so many enemies, we screwed up a lot of people.

It was The Stranglers' struggle for recognition and respect that formed the underlying theme for their confrontational, speed-fuelled second album, *No More Heroes*, which was released in September 1977, just six months after the debut *Rattus Norvegicus*. Recorded in 14 days, once more with producer Martin Rushent, it documented the violent maelstrom that had surrounded their career so far.

The record kicked off with the incendiary "I Feel Like A Wog", which documented the band's dangerous encounter with a pimp in the red light district of Hamburg. As Cornwell was to relate:

He wanted to take us down to an area of Hamburg called St. Pauli, but we didn't have any money. We tried to get on his good side so we could get some freebies and I told him a surrealist joke, but he just said I was mad. We'd been getting on well with him, but he suddenly started thinking we were odd and made us feel alienated.

Although the song was intended to be anti-racist, Cornwell noting that its message was *"that you don't have to be black to be made to feel foreign"*, it was initially condemned for its use of the perjorative word "wog". This was no "Melting Pot" or "Ebony and Ivory", no attempt to pour oil over troubled waters. Instead it is an abrasive statement of difference. Rather than emphasizing how we're all the same under the skin, it employs race as a metaphor for alienation:

I feel like a wog
People give me the eyes
But I was born here just like you

In the After Eight club, when *Pimpo* tells Cornwell that he isn't right in the head, we feel that awful void open up when we realise that somebody doesn't like us not for what we've said, or what we've done, but for what we are. It is our very essence that is objected to. There is nothing we can change about ourselves to bridge the chasm. On another level, despite the lyrics being Cornwell's, there is the sense that he is singing on behalf of Burnel, that the word "wog" is merely a placeholder for "frog". As Burnel was to tell Gary Kent:

I was still fresh from being called a wog or frog at school. A bit rich as I was born in London, I'm a Londoner. I was born in St. Mary Abbotts, the same hospital Jimi Hendrix died.

If joining the Stranglers had gone some way to ameliorating the sense of separation that Burnel had felt from being considered foreign, it was simultaneously aggravated by the rejection the group had received from their peers. Within the punk subculture, the band themselves were now the "wogs", and once again it was Burnel who was particularly affected. Being the youngest member of the band, and the same age as Clash singer Joe Strummer, he felt the greatest affinity with the punk scene whereas the older members could accept their ostracisation with varying degrees of pragmatism. Cornwell viewed the situation equivocally:

Because we missed that pub rock thing – we were too young and not good enough to be a part of it – the pub rock musicians sneered at us. And then when the punk thing happened we were too good and too old. So we were this misanthropic group between the two. And that stayed with us. We were a class of one.

"Dead Ringer" was the band's musical response to their peers. Sung, or rather sneered, by Dave Greenfield, it pointed an accusatory finger at the denizens of this supposedly spontaneous new scene. As Cornwell noted:

At this time there were a lot of people resurfacing whom we'd seen before in other guises, who had suddenly adopted the punk ethic and look. We thought 'hang on a minute, you've changed your image and your politics so that you're in fashion'.

The ghoulish riff and taunting lyrics likened the punk scene to a playground, whose inhabitants were akin to the kids who cheated at the school-yard game of conkers (*"conkeroonee stringers"*). The line *"wasn't it you running round proud of being poor?"* was clearly aimed at Joe Strummer of The Clash, a former squatter, as well as that band's guitarist Mick Jones, who had claimed never to have lived lower than the 18th floor of a tower block.

Ultimately, the uneasy relationship The Stranglers had with the punk scene reflected the need that the various protagonists within the movement had for authenticity. In *The Culture Of Narcissism*, the contemporary social critic Christopher Lasch had noticed that in the late-industrial cultures of the West, in which basic needs had become easily satisfied, and new wants had to be created by the propaganda of advertising, a "cult of authenticity" had emerged within "the spectacle" of consumerism that fetishised spontaneity and the confessional. Punk's most glaring, and therefore most sensitive, internal contradiction was that it was a largely manufactured movement that was intended to give vent to the organic, spontaneous rage of British youth. It is one of the sacred precepts of punk's apologists that it was inevitable, that "the kids" were just waiting for something to happen. Punk's most overt narcissist, the Sex Pistols' manager Malcolm McLaren, was to retrospectively credit himself not with inventing punk, but with facilitating it, with channeling the outpouring like the director of a sewage works.

The Stranglers were both more authentic than the other punks – they had been around longer, they had taken the knocks – but also less so. Their public relations man Alan Edwards made no bones about how he had positioned the group to take advantage of the mushrooming scene:

Their relationship with punk was a bit forced, they were more psychedelic warriors with a punk attitude. We pushed them that way, starting the fanzine 'Strangled' and positioning them alongside The Clash in the media.

The Stranglers weren't marginalised because their "opportunism" made them less "real" than the other punk groups. They were marginalised because their established history drew attention to the inauthenticity of the others. For Burnel, this was intolerable:

We were much more violent than any of the other bands because we'd developed a missionary attitude. I wasn't going to let anyone bottle me off stage. In 1976 we did 300 gigs and we were fighting every other night. The other bands were getting the hip press and playing loft parties but we were on the front line. Barricaded in our dressing room in Glasgow. Beaten to a pulp in North Wales. The punks who followed us knew we weren't the 'real thing', but the real thing was phonier. Mick Jones and all the other guys used to come and see us when they had long hair.

Hugh Cornwell, on the other hand, took a more detached view:

The punk bands were very distrustful. They couldn't work us out. They didn't know whether to be scared by us, we just weren't of their group. Too philosophical, too much intelligence, keyboards ...

ooh, that's dodgy, can't trust them, they've got a keyboard player with long hair and a moustache. It was all silly stuff like this. Privately, I had quite a good relationship with Joe Strummer. Paul and Steve from the Sex Pistols would come to the gigs, talk to Jet about drumming and stuff. So there was private contact, but not public. But it didn't bother me, because I understood. Punk had all these rules you weren't allowed to transgress, and if you did you were banished. And that's one of the reasons why we thought it was all a bit of a sham. But one can understand why it had to be so strict, because it was peddling its own hype. It had to have these strict edges in order for it to be seen, to be in focus. It had to be defined like that.

What this confirmed was that punk as performance wasn't limited to what happened on the stage. It conformed to Lasch's notion of *"the theatre of everyday life"*, the *"sense of self as a performer under the constant scrutiny of friends and strangers"* in a *"society pervaded by symbolically mediated information."* This in turn fed punk's second prominent internal contradiction: its apparent yearning for spontaneity had created a subculture replete with social and behavioural taboos. In a dominant culture where advertising and the image were all-pervasive, punk's attempt to displace those images couldn't escape the mirror world that surrounded it, where *"actors and spectators alike ... seek reassurance of our capacity to captivate or impress others, anxiously searching out blemishes that might detract from the appearance we intend to project."*

Punk's liberating power derived to a great degree in allowing its adherents the creative freedom to self-define entirely new identities. These identities, always precarious in their gestation, could be richly metaphorical; ripped shirts alluded to holes in the social fabric, bondage trousers symbolised social and sexual oppression, pseudonyms evoked everything from voided person-alities to romantic poets. But the fragility of these identities was in great part a source of the violent energy that initially powered the scene. They had to be fought for and aggressively defended. If punk had its stylistic conventions, it was nevertheless incumbent on any putative recruit to find a distinctive persona that couldn't be attributed to plagiarism. It would be this principle that would provoke the event that definitively estranged The Stranglers from their peers.

On July 5th 1976, the group supported The Ramones and The Flamin' Groovies at an American Bicentennial celebration concert at the Roundhouse theatre. This in itself was viewed as a prestigious booking, indicating that The Stranglers were becoming viewed as the premier London punk band, especially after a News Of The World exposé three months earlier had identified them as among the leaders of the new youth cult. At an after-show party at the nearby Dingwalls club, attended by many of the most prominent punk musicians, Burnel assaulted Paul Simonon of The Clash. As he was to recall:

In those days Paul had this nervous tic where he used to spit, y'know, Hey don't I look cool – spit. He did it as I walked past and I thought he was spitting at me, so I thumped him in the gut.

Simonon fell back on Steve Jones and Paul Cook, and as the clientele piled outside, a stand-off ensued between The Stranglers with some of their supporters, and the combined members of The Sex Pistols and The Clash and their entourages. Notable cameos included Dave Greenfield hauling John Lydon up against the side of a transit van, and Cornwell and Strummer dryly commentating in the background as Burnel and Simonon sized each other up. Although the incident quickly petered out, it would mark the watershed moment when The Stranglers became outcasts even within this marginal scene. As Sex Pistols bassist Glen Matlock was to recall:

I remember doing a Pistols photo shoot on Denmark Street when J.J. Burnel sped by, 'Wotcha!' he called out. I said something cordial in reply, and Johnny Rotten turned to me and said: 'You don't talk to people like that, do you?'

And yet, there was more to the Dingwalls incident than first meets the eye. It is unlikely that Burnel selected Simonon for attack as coincidentally as he suggested. Firstly, like Burnel, the Clash man was a leather jacket wearing, heart-throb bass player who liked to adopt striking poses while onstage. Secondly, Simonon is a French surname. It is difficult to avoid the suspicion that, either consciously or unconsciously, Burnel felt that Simonon was stealing his identity, and that this was the under-lying provocation. When Jean Jacques Burnel assaulted Paul Gustave Simonon, he was, to an extent, attacking himself, or at least a facsimile of himself. Indeed, the uncanny affinity between the two men is evidenced by their rapprochement decades later, when they stopped to admire each others Triumph motorbikes at a junction in London.

Like a sorcerer's apprentice, however, Burnel's action only seemed to create more doppelgängers, one of whom emerged when Sid Vicious replaced Matlock as the Sex Pistols' bass player. Although the Pistols themselves had succeeded in causing outrage, it had hitherto carried the aura of grotesquerie rather than real physical threat. They lacked the dark aura of danger that The Stranglers projected. Worse, Lydon aside, their boyishness wasn't particularly photogenic, which was one of the reasons they had to rely so heavily on Jamie Reid's graphics. The purpose of enlisting Vicious was to give the band their own iconic, schizo-violent danger man, their own JJ Burnel. And, there was no disputing that Sid, neé John Simon Ritchie, looked magnificent, especially onstage. Unfortunately, he couldn't play his instrument, and, in the words of Lydon, *"couldn't punch his way out of a wet paper bag"*. The whole farrago was a characteristic piece of McLaren extemporisation, and it only served to emphasise what a jerry-built institution the Sex Pistols were.

However, it was sonically that Burnel was to find his identity endlessly replicated. If the sound of his bass guitar was an unmistakable signifier of presence, a sound that stated unambiguously "I AM", then it was musically also a signpost to the future. If post-punk was nothing else, it was a couple of hundred variably successful attempts to replicate The Stranglers' bass sound. The politics of the time meant that this could not be acknowledged, but later Peter Hook of Joy Division was to explain to DJ Ron Slomowicz:

> I mean, I love early Jean Jacques Burnel, from The Stranglers; he was my hero. I aspired to be like him. A lot of the equipment I bought was Jean Jacques' equipment. I was just watching myself playing ... using the Hiwatt amp; I bought the Hiwatt amp because Jean Jacques had one. That's funny, isn't it? It does work, doesn't it, when you buy peoples' equipment.

There can rarely have been an occasion where a musician has been held in such generalised contempt by his emulators, and this was due to the pernicious dynamic in which Burnel found himself: his style provoked emulation, yet his identity was so tenuous that he was compelled to respond violently to those he felt were encroaching on it. This generated a fear and loathing that ensured that his influence went unacknowledged, which in turn fed the deepening sense of persecution and paranoia that was to eventually overwhelm The Stranglers.

Burnel's aggression at Dingwalls was partly brought on by his inebriation, thanks to a bottle of wine that had been provided by the band's biggest fan and mentor at the time, Dagenham Dave. According to Hugh Cornwell:

*Dave was originally from Manchester, but worked at the Ford
factory at Dagenham on the production line and was a very vocal
shop steward. He was a working-class bloke, extremely intelligent
and spoke up about conditions at the plant. I think he was sacked in
the end. He then became a scaffolder, which was very well paid, so he
didn't have to work a lot.*

Dave was also of an immigrant background, being partly West
Indian, and the sheer fanaticism of his support for the band (on
one occasion he even offered them his girlfriend) suggests that he
fundamentally understood the source of the maelstrom of
violence that enveloped them. He too was searching for an
identity within The Stranglers, and for him the search was to
prove fatal. As with Burnel and so many other people whose
identity is precarious, whether due to their ethnic origin,
uncertain family background, or divergent sexuality, Dave was
an autodidact.

Autodidacticism is so often a restless search for knowledge in
the evasion of an uncomfortable truth. It is a search for the source
of a person's alienation in social theory and social history; an
attempt to construct a neutral framework to explain to oneself
that the source of one's isolation is due to hostile external forces,
political, ideological, hegemonic, but most of all artificial. What it
attempts to avoid is the conclusion that instead the reason may
actually be organic, and therefore almost impossible to rectify:
you don't belong because you don't belong. And the reason you
don't belong is because you are at least partly foreign, or because
not knowing who one or both of your parents were opens up a
social void where no roots can take hold. For a second-generation
immigrant such as Burnel, this was a particularly agonising
dilemma, as the second generation migrant is at the moment of
greatest equipoise between the parent and the adopted culture.

Burnel paid his dues to Dagenham Dave's erudition on the
eponymous tribute to him on "No More Heroes", in which the

scaffolder *"had read De Sade to Marx; read more than me or you"*. The song itself alternated between an unsentimental, almost triumphant evocation of a fallen fellow warrior, and a bleak description of the loneliness of urban life. It was a scabrous postscript to the melancholia of "Waterloo Sunset". As Ray Davies' dirty old river rolls into the night, the abandoned and alienated throw themselves in. *"The River Thames is cold; it keeps on flowing on"* Burnel observed indignantly.

Before his corpse was pulled out of the mud of the Thames in February 1977, Dagenham Dave had provided The Stranglers with invaluable moral and financial support. Introducing himself to the group after a set at The Golden Lion in the summer of 1976, he would demonstrate his belief in the band by attending every gig he could, keeping them and their road crew fed and watered, and providing them with places to stay. He would spend up to £50 an evening, a substantial sum at the time, ensuring that the group didn't suffer any shortfalls from poorly-attended or low-paying gigs. A coal-miner's son, Dave was also a formidable physical presence, and, like Burnel, had a tendency to be behaviorally schizoid: relaxed and cheerful at one moment, dangerously violent the next. Indeed, there was a curious similarity between the two men; they were both intelligent and sensitive enough to appreciate classical music, and in Dave's case jazz (he was a fan of Charlie Parker) and yet both were equally happy taking on multiple opponents in a brawl.

Although Dave was convinced that The Stranglers were going to be a huge success, he didn't appreciate that as the band were bound to pick up more admirers, these would inevitably displace him from his intimate position with the group. It was the arrival of a young, aggressive cadre of fans, the Finchley Boys, that was to seal his fate. It was during a gig at the Torrington Arms in November 1976 that the Finchleys were first encountered. As they warmed up for their set, the band noticed a group of more than a dozen fierce-looking young men enter the venue, and head straight for the toilets, where they disappeared for a few minutes, only to emerge dressed as punks; a scheme they had devised to evade the censorious door staff. The young lads quickly showed how much they appreciated The Stranglers' music, and a strong bond was formed between the two groups that would flower into a kind of mutual-appreciation-and-destruction relationship over the coming year.

In effect, the Finchley Boys were to form a kind of Praetorian guard in front of the band as they gigged up and down the country, playing towns and cities where other London-based groups hardly dared to venture. They were even supplied with their own identifying t-shirts by The Stranglers' management, confirming their status within the band's overall organisation. The Boys had their own transport, an aged grey Ford Transit nicknamed "ROD" in which they would endeavor to attend every concert, no matter how far away, or how unwelcoming the locals might be. And, as their notoriety increased with that of the band themselves, some destinations would be very hostile indeed. Many gigs descended into chaos, with the mordant Cornwell invariably acting as the verbal provocateur, while Burnel and the Finchleys attempted to physically deal with the result. As Burnel himself remembered:

> In those days it was always The Stranglers against everybody else, but people deserved to be provoked if they were stupid. We did a gig for anti-nuclear power, and Hugh said: "It's very nice to be here supporting nuclear power." Of course it all went off.

The confrontation between the Finchley Boys and Dagenham Dave happened at the 100 Club a fortnight after the gig at the Torrington, when a heavily inebriated Dave attempted to take on his new rivals en masse, and received a beating that left him in hospital nursing broken ribs and a fractured skull. The ruckus was punctuated by the arrival of Malcolm McLaren and the then

Stranglers' manager Dai Davies, who was attempting to persuade McLaren to include his band on the forthcoming "Anarchy In The UK" tour. The Sex Pistols manager was overcome by an uncharacteristic moment of public concern and vetoed Davies' proposal.

Although there were attempts made at a reconciliation with the Finchleys, it was the beginning of the end for Dagenham Dave, who embarked on the path of dissolution that would end with his suicide. The Finchley Boys themselves would also find themselves immortalised on *No More Heroes*, on the song "Burning Up Time", which celebrated the speed-fueled milieu in which the band found themselves:

The weekend's here the Finchley Boys
Are gonna make a lot of noise
It's burning up time

Cornwell's ferocious riff, and the chorus itself, underlined that the combustible relationship the band had with their fans and audience at this time could only be temporary; that it would soon burn itself out. Indeed, having your own private army, which is what the Finchley Boys amounted to, presented all kinds of dangers, some of which would manifest themselves when another punk band followed The Stranglers' lead.

Whereas the appearance of the Finchley Boys had been entirely fortuitous, Sham 69 went out of their way to cultivate a fan base that corporately identified themselves with the band; their own "Sham Army". If the search for meaning and identity, and its manifestation through violence, is what attracted the waifs and strays to The Stranglers, then the missionary Jimmy Pursey, Sham's singer and songwriter, went out looking to gather them into his fold.

The Finchley Boys had been characterised by BBC Radio as *"a hooligan outfit more suited to football terraces than music venues"*, and with songs such as "If The Kids Are United" and "Hersham Boys", Sham 69 put terrace chants to music in an attempt to bring together Britain's disparate youth tribes. The result can fairly be described as disastrous, as the band soon attracted the noxious attention of the far-Right, who began to attend, and, when made unwelcome, disrupt, the group's concerts. Pursey had become another sorcerer's apprentice, far more inept than Burnel, and his idealistic attempt to somehow "unite" the youth could only be prevented from turning iatrogenic by the premature disbandment of Sham 69 themselves.

The rise of football hooliganism and violent youth cultures, tentatively in the 1950s, then explosively from the mid-1960s onwards, was a manifestation of the breakdown of organic solidarity within British life, which again reflected the general malaise of national decline, with the absence of the unifying purpose of Empire and the consequent demise of industry, and its identity-defining occupations. The British, once more or less a tribe, and defined by their external competitors and enemies, had become tribal, defining themselves regionally, generationally, and by consumer taste. Only class differences had remained largely unchanged, but these had never greatly affected how the nation projected itself internationally. Nevertheless, if the reasons for this fracturing of identity lay in specifically British causes, we shall see later how the conditions for their expression in "uproars" like punk were defined by a pan-Western unease.

There was yet another "tribe" that The Stranglers became associated with during this period, and with whom their relationship, though often close, would become treacherously uneasy: the Hells Angels. The Stranglers first encountered the Dutch chapter of the notorious motorcycle gang during a gig at the Paradiso Club in Amsterdam in September 1977. At first, the group interpreted the phalanx of threatening figures that were starting to position themselves around the edge of the stage as precipitating an attack, but it soon transpired that the Angels had appointed themselves as stage security, tidily dispatching any teenage fans who were making a nuisance of themselves. When the concert had finished, the Angels followed the group backstage, and invited them to visit their own private bar within the city, The Other Place, where the bikers' wives and girlfriends worked as prostitutes.

From there, the Angels took the group to their complex on the outskirts of the city, whose construction had been subsidised by the Dutch government, who also allocated each member of the club an annual living allowance. The authorities presumably did this to mitigate their behaviour, although to what extent this was achieved is uncertain. The Stranglers were shown the tripod-mounted machine gun the Angels kept in their back garden, which was used to take pot shots at a prison complex being constructed next door. Other entertainments included the projection of a series of films featuring the bikers engaging in various acts of sex and violence, and the offer of sleeping with the Angels' partners, which was apparently their ultimate gesture of respect to a guest. This example of women-as-potlatch had of course been prefigured by Dagenham Dave, and though, according to Cornwell, the band had once again declined the offer, it demonstrated the kind of anti-structural behaviour that, consciously or unconsciously, the group tended to attract.

There can be no doubt that the Hells Angels found The Stranglers' predatory antinomianism deeply resonant, and, initially at least, the band responded with an equal fascination for the Angels' lifestyle. In a terse interview with Melody Maker in June 1978, Cornwell attempted to justify the behaviour of the Amsterdam chapter, who had been implicated in ever more frequent assaults on the audiences at punk gigs:

They've got about the only culture which is alternative, they've got their own community which lives outside of the law. The law leaves them alone, and they leave the law alone.

This romantic view of the Hells Angels lifestyle had first been advanced on the song "Bitching" on *No More Heroes,* in which Burnel contrasted the back-biting of the London punk scene, and the indifferent treatment the group had received at the hands of promoters, with the fraternal welcome that had been extended by the Angels:

> *I'll tell you what we'll meet in Amsterdam*
> *And then you'll see what should be really can*

It was Burnel who was most taken with the Hells Angels, which was no surprise as his enthusiasm for motorcycling had previously brought him into contact with another biker gang in Surrey. *"They glorify individuality and freedom, but individuality within the pack"* he stated during the same interview:

> *In a way they're living out their ideals. And also we were the first people who weren't intimidated by them, so they thought 'great, we don't have to bully these people'.*

Burnel was equally enthused by the Angels' indifferent treatment of their female partners; how their economic use as prostitutes allowed the gang to augment their state-funded lifestyle, granting them unlimited time to indulge in their own esoteric pursuits. The underlying attraction here was one of immersion in the undifferentiated corporate identity of the group. To be an Angel was to be the ultimate insider among the ultimate outsiders. The denigration of women in this context was a strategy to ensure that all demonstrations of affection were homosocial, that the spark of individualism couldn't be ignited by the idiosyncrasy inherent in romantic love. It was this yearning for the erasure of the individual within the congregation that would inspire Burnel's controversial interest in the Japanese writer and revolutionary Yukio Mishima.

The Stranglers' relationships with both the Finchley Boys and the Hells Angels would attenuate from 1978 onwards, as the band's success saw them playing larger and more impersonal venues, whose more professional organisation marginalised any dubious supplementary role those groups could adopt. Also, the Stranglers' own music had become colder and more abstract, as the blood-red throb of their first two albums turned monochrome. As the close male bonds that the Finchleys and the Angels offered started to retreat into the distance, so Burnel's interest in Mishima came to the fore.

Yukio Mishima had committed ritual suicide after an attempted coup at the barracks of the Tokyo headquarters of the Japanese Self-Defence Forces in November 1970. This highly theatrical gesture, in which he and four members of his own private army, the Tatenokai, had stormed onto the camp commandant's balcony in order to proclaim their manifesto to restore the power and divinity of the Emperor, was treated with jeering disdain by the soldiers below. It had brought a premature end to the contradictory career of this most perplexing artist, who had produced a torrent of novels, poems and plays during his relatively short life, as well as directing and acting in his own films.

Born in 1925 in the Yotsuya district of Tokyo to parents related to, but not of, the *daimyo*, the second most elite group of families in Japan, Mishima was separated from his parents during early childhood and brought up by his grandmother, Natsu, who maintained aristocratic pretensions and shielded him from contact with both sunlight and other boys. His time was spent either alone or with his female cousins and their dolls. At six years old he was enrolled in the elite *Gakushuin*, or Peer's School, normally reserved for the *kuge*, Japan's imperial class, and at twelve he became the youngest member of the editorial board of its literary society. It was also at this time that he was returned to the care of his parents, and it was both at home and at school where the schisms in his character were to emerge. An avid admirer of the work of such "decadent" Western writers as Radiguet, Wilde and Rilke, he attracted the scorn of his militaristic father as well as of the school's rugby union team, to which he belonged.

During the Second World War Mishima had been humiliatingly declared unfit for military service, but had continued writing against his father's express wishes. After graduating from the University of Tokyo in 1947, and following a final struggle with his father, he dedicated himself to writing, and began a series of semi-autobiographical novels, such as "Confessions Of A Mask" and "Forbidden Colours" in which he documented the intense inner conflicts that his repressed homosexuality provoked within the conformist culture of Japan.

In essence, Mishima's work was concerned with the paradoxes of masculinity, and it is easy to see why it would be appealing to Burnel. Indeed Mishima's own life had deep parallels with that of Burnel, as well as that of Nicky Crane. In the case of all three men, we can see a nexus of violence, male bonding, homosexuality, and childhood alienation. However, to understand it we need to look at the work of a fourth man, who like Mishima, had also endured a difficult and remote childhood: the Austrian psychoanalyst and psychotherapist Alfred Adler.

Burnel's paean to Mishima, "Death And Night And Blood", whose title was taken from "Confessions Of A Mask", appeared on The Stranglers' third album, 1978's *Black And White*. Segued onto the end of "Do You Wanna", a sardonic appraisal of female career options sung by Dave Greenfield, it is perhaps the very nadir of the band's journey into the darkest regions of the irrational. Opening with an agonising roar of bass, like a Mastodon flailing in a tar pit, it presents a queasy melange of Fascist and misogynist imagery, in which a tableau of torch-lit parades is juxtaposed with a depiction of submissive fellatio: the feminine instinct utterly subordinated to the masculine will. The chorus is explicit in its horror of femininity:

Hey little baby don't you lean down low
Your brain's exposed and you're starting to show
Your rotten thoughts, yuk!

As Burnel himself was to explain, the rejection of the feminine necessarily meant that libidinal energy must be directed elsewhere:

That's a chorus about women and it's very much a part of Yukio ...
he was a homosexual – in the best possible warrior way, like the
Spartans, the Samurai, and Alexander the Great's guard. It was an
integral part of their warriorhood, of being very close to fellow
warriors. It has to be like that, because you don't take women to war
with you.

Nevertheless, no matter how unusual this line of thinking may first appear, it conforms very closely with a series of concepts that Adler developed in his model of the development of the individual. These concepts are the "inferiority complex", the "superiority complex", "compensation", and most particularly of all, what he called "masculine protest".

Adler was, along with Sigmund Freud and Carl Jung, one of the founding fathers of psychoanalysis, though his reputation in modern times has somewhat diminished in comparison to the other two, which is curious as he was in many ways the most perceptive and profound of the trio. In his schema of development, the inferiority complex inevitably emerges in all individuals in childhood simply as a consequence of the child's helplessness and dependence on adults, especially parents, on account of their comparative physical and mental weakness. However, this sense of inferiority can be exacerbated by such circumstances as physical deformity or illness, parental or social neglect, or social discrimination based on gender, ethnicity or class, amongst others.

Adler believed that individuals attempt to overcome their innate sense of inferiority by some kind of compensation. For healthy individuals this generally means becoming gregariously involved in society and overcoming the social fear engendered by other individuals. However, for those who suffer from an exaggerated feeling of inferiority, whether subjective or more or less objective, then there is a tendency for overcompensation, to replace the inferiority complex with a superiority complex.

Masculine protest is therefore a culturally accepted, sometimes culturally privileged, form of overcompensation against the inferiority complex, which is itself identified as "feminine" due to it provoking "unmanly" feelings of dependence, submission and obedience. Instead of the urge for compensation being routed in social activities that can abate the sense of inferiority, masculine protest channels it into aggression, compulsion, ambition and, in Adler's words, *"posits for itself the highest and often unattainable goals"*. The result is a schismatic individual, with *"the often ramified feminine traits carefully hidden by hypertrophied masculine wishes and efforts."*

We can see therefore, not only how Mishima's weight training and warrior ethos could co-exist with his sensual artistry and homoeroticism, but how they were mutually dependent upon one another, just as were Crane's fascist violence and closet homosexuality. Their sense of childhood isolation exaggerated their feelings of inferiority, which were overcompensated for with the ultimate manifestations of masculine protest: fascism and self-sacrifice.

"Death And Night And Blood" is a truly colossal expression of masculine protest, one of the most brutal pieces of rock music ever recorded, but the "little baby" who is leaning down low is not a real woman; it is Burnel's own femininity, his own hidden sense of inferiority. The song is a psychodrama, just as was the work of Mishima himself. It is one of the landmarks in Burnel's journey to resolve his own internal contradictions.

To a great extent, rock music itself is a primary expression of masculine protest, and as such it is no surprise that it is often at its most misogynistic when it is at its most effeminate. The long hair, make-up and gamine movements of the Rolling Stones, Led Zeppelin and their ilk were the natural counterpoint to the violent machismo of their songs. However, rock music was not the only avenue for Burnel's own masculine protest. As well as his interest in motorcycles, he was a black belt in Shidokan karate, which he would frequently deploy in his hair-trigger responses to real or perceived slights. As Adler had said of masculine protest, it finds *"disparagement, and injury unbearable. Defiance, vengeance and resentment are its steady accompaniments."* Nor was Burnel a stranger to homosexuality; his conquests included the scenester and Visage frontman Steve Strange, though his later recollection of the encounter was less than poetic. As he told John Robb:

> *I shagged the arse of him literally and it was great from what I remember. I didn't make a habit of it. But it was there so I took it. He told me he was from Wales so I thought that's fine and I put my wellies on and away you go.*

Nevertheless, Japan was to retain a fascination for Burnel. Its cultural unity and order, no matter how alien, contrasted deeply with his own identity, split between England and France, both of whose own idiosyncratic cultures were under continual assault from across the Atlantic. On the band's 1979 album, *The Raven*, Burnel would contribute "Ice", a darkly inscrutable song that referenced the Hagakure, an eighteenth century samurai code, which had been written during a period when Japanese society was transitioning to a more stable and therefore peaceful order, and in which the old warrior class were becoming bureaucratized. One of its themes was how to die an honourable death in a society in which personal honour was becoming less important.

If Mishima's masculine protest was against his innate femininity, it was also against a rationalising order which not only bureaucratized and feminised, but also infantilised. As Burnel put it in an interview with the NME the same year:

The day he committed suicide – seppuku – he was urging them to throw off their American shackles and regain their national self-respect. During the samurai days being a trader, a businessman, was the lowest of the low – it was much lower than being a peasant. Money was totally obscene.

The Stranglers' anti-Americanism was strident even by the standards of British punk, but what set the band apart from their contemporaries in this respect was that they didn't diplomatically quell or temper their opinions of the USA even when they visited that country. In fact, they did quite the opposite. As Hugh Cornwell was to inform Creem magazine:

Well we hated America before we even got here ... because we'd had American culture rammed down our throats since we were small. And we felt a bit repressed about it and a bit resentful of it.

The band's early tours of America were so brief, and so full of invective toward their hosts, that they almost gave the impression that their very purpose was simply to insult and upset the locals, with promoting their career or entertaining their fans coming a distant second. Chris Salewicz of the NME reported a diatribe that Cornwell delivered to a New York journalist:

You have all got smaller brains. Just a bit lacking in the old cerebellum, that's all. You may rule the Western hemisphere but you're pretty incompetent in any ruling of the cerebral hemispheres. Actually, I think that's why you're so fanatical about taking over all the other hemispheres. Because you're all so lacking upstairs.

The idea of Americans literally having smaller brains had first been mooted, by all appearances seriously, by Burnel in an interview with Melody Maker in 1978, and the controversy that this caused followed them across the Atlantic, provoking a number of hostile incidents, and resulting in the group having to be escorted from the premises of a Boston radio station by armed police. Burnel had been recalling their first fleeting visit to the USA the previous year:

There was nothing there we could appreciate, nothing in the American culture that appealed to our superior Europeanism. They had nothing to offer us and we had so much to offer them. Most people seem to have an inferiority complex and think America is better, which is an amazing result of post-war brainwashing because everyone knows that Americans have got smaller brains. Fact of life, you know, they're just inferior specimens.

It was comments such as this, augmenting the band's already dubious reputation for misogyny and violence, that led to most of the prominent US journalists taking a leaf from their British counterparts in ostracising them. The influential Village Voice critic Robert Christgau took a leading role, as Cornwell related:

He did that because he was so outraged at our lyrics, apparently, and when we heard about that we sent him a telegram saying, 'If you're not careful we're going to come round and slip your wife some real British beef'. And he totally freaked out. It all seems very self-righteous.

Not even the group's American record label escaped their self-sabotaging ardour. A proposal by A&M to raise their Stateside profile by releasing a sampler LP of tracks from their first two albums met with the memorable telegrammed response:

DEAR A&M RECORDS GET FUCKED LOVE FROM THE STRANGLERS

Which would later be framed and mounted above the reception desk in the company's Los Angeles office. Nevertheless, The Stranglers' seeming antipathy to the home of rock'n'roll appeared on one level to be motivated by a certain amount of pragmatism. As Burnel was to later reflect:

> *At one point we were the biggest selling band in the UK, bigger than The Clash and the Pistols. Those bands did the smart thing – like The Police and a few other bands like Flock Of Seagulls, all these bands decided to go round America until you break it. The Clash started wearing Stetsons and cowboy boots, but we could never sound American … we were very much a British band and America didn't suit us.*

But mixed within this apparent pragmatism was once again an overriding concern with maintaining identity. For The Stranglers, as with any other foreign group, Stateside success necessarily brought with it the implied commitment to dilute any indigenous components that may have informed their music. And this is what motivates much anti-Americanism the world over: American culture (as perhaps would any dominant culture) acts as a solvent that erodes the idiosyncrasies of any local culture that it infiltrates, dissolving individual identities in its path. It is a possibility, though one seldom considered by those who promote it, that the USA's vaunted "soft power" ultimately provokes more hostility than the worst errors of its foreign policy. However, The Stranglers' "Britishness" was far from being a fixed, parochial marker of distinction. For Burnel especially, it was a token that presaged a greater, European identity, one that he was to elaborate with his first solo album, *Euroman Cometh*, released in April 1979.

If the post-war years had witnessed the signal decline of Britain and its economic fortunes, then they had also seen quite the opposite phenomenon emerge within western continental Europe. The European Economic Community, created by the 1957 Treaty of Rome between signatories Belgium, France, Italy, Luxembourg, the Netherlands and West Germany, was a supranational body that had tasked itself with the economic integration of its members in order to further their economic interests, and, as a by-product, reduce the likelihood of a future European war. In contrast to Britain, the opening up of this European customs union had helped facilitate Germany's *"Wirtschaftswunder"* and France's *"Trente Glorieuses"*, economic miracles that had contrasted tellingly with the fortunes of what was now considered "the sick man of Europe".

Britain had initially rejected the invitation to join the EEC, somewhat haughtily considering its Commonwealth trade links as offering greater economic prospects, and its capitulation to American pressure during the Suez crisis had led the French in particular to view it as too subordinate to United States' influence to be a reliable European partner. Consequently the French president Charles De Gaulle had spent the 1960s continually vetoing the UK's belated attempts to gain membership. By the time Britain had eventually clawed its way to full membership, it had been so forced to compromise its position on such key issues as the Common Agricultural Policy (which it perceived to be scandalously weighted in the interests of French farmers) and the trade preferences it had formerly granted to its Commonwealth partners (which would be a lingering sore with the Antipodean nations particularly) that there could be no doubt that it would never be a contented member of the "Common Market", even if such a relationship had ever been possible.

Nevertheless, most Britons viewed the acquisition of EEC membership with optimism, none more so than Jean Jacques

Burnel, and *Euroman Cometh* was his personal response. It is an extraordinary record in that almost every aspect of its conception is didactic. The idiosyncratic exposition of the European future that it envisaged allowed Burnel to employ his Adlerian superiority complex in the service of annealing his fractured identity. Britain entering "Europe", as the EEC was colloquially called, provided a healing macro-identity within which his schizoid Anglo-French persona could more comfortably nestle. Not only that, but Burnel's ideological differences with the EEC allowed him to present himself as the man of destiny that Europe had long been awaiting; The Gubernator who would finally lead Europa on the correct path from which its previous Great Men had erred.

The album cover depicts Burnel standing in front of the functionalist monolith of the recently opened Centre Georges Pompidou in Paris, significant not only because it represented an unsentimentally modern and forward looking Europe, but also because it was a prestigious building in France co-designed by an Englishman of European descent (the Italian-born Richard Rogers, in partnership with Renzo Piano) and also because Pompidou was the French president who had acquiesced to British membership of the EEC. The building, with its nerves and sinews boldly mounted externally, provided an equally appropriate metaphor for the music contained within – it was as much a didactic form as Burnel's arrangements, which, being influenced by the inimically European likes of Can and Kraftwerk, went out of their way to avoid popular American idioms, an approach Burnel confirmed expressly, in French, on the track "Euroman".

"Euroman" opened with Burnel declaring himself to be a descendent of Charlemagne, Cromwell, Napoleon and Hitler, and the inner sleeve of the record presented a series of maps that depict the various Europes that each of these great bad men had conceived, as well as maps of the "Soviet Europe" that lay behind the Iron Curtain, and the Europe of the EEC. The message that this collection of charts presents is clear – neither the strong men of history, nor the contemporary bureaucratised institutions that replicated their power in the post-war world, had the might or vision to truly forge a United States of Europe. Worse, it had taken until the advent of the EEC for the crucial union to be brought into being – that of England and France. If Burnel posited himself as the descendent of Europe's failed unifiers, he did so on the assumption that he was the man to do the job properly, even if at the present time that could only mean defining the vision correctly.

The single taken from the record, "Freddie Laker (Concorde and Eurobus)", was an explicitly anti-American tirade directed at what Burnel saw as the deliberate attempts by US manufacturers to sabotage the European aircraft industry. The song chronicles the controversy surrounding the protests aimed at banning the supersonic airliner Concorde from landing at American airports because of its alleged high noise levels and tendency to create sonic booms. Concorde was iconic not only for its advanced concept, but because it was an example of Anglo-French collaboration, which would of course have been particularly piquant for the Stranglers' bassist. These protests were notably ill-received in Europe, as it was suspected that at worst they were being covertly organised by the American airliner manufacturers Boeing and McDonnell Douglas, and at best were an unsporting demonstration of sour grapes from a nation that had failed to meet the same technical challenge.

For Burnel, they were an overt example of the bad faith that the USA demonstrated towards Europe, one that shone a light on the more covert string-pulling it was engaged in to suppress European ambitions. The answer lay in the new "Eurobus", later to become familiar as Airbus, that pooled European manufacturing resources, and created the continent-wide market that the American businesses had utilised to crush the previous ambitions of British and French aircraft makers, the British in particular having had a sorry record in the civil aviation market.

The song elevates Freddie Laker, a charismatic entrepreneur who tried to break the cartel of transatlantic airline companies by offering discounted air fares, in the process becoming something of a British popular hero, into a mythic figure battling the grey men of the corporations. *"Freddie Laker epitomised the lengths the Americans would go to fuck over the European"*, Burnel would later assert. The song itself demonstrated the harsh anti-naturalism that pervaded the album from which it was culled. It's a thrilling piece of music, anchored by a clean, resonant bassline and featuring a careering guitar solo from John Ellis of The Vibrators, yet it employs an unusual use of the vocoder; instead of adding lubricity to the vocals in the manner usually employed by American funksters, it creates a kind of mechanical howl, like a jet engine spooling over heated tarmac. Combined with Penny Tobin's whooshing keyboards, it pushed the song away from popular taste and firmly into the field of the experimental.

The industrial theme continued with "Triumph Of The Good City", a tribute to the Triumph Workers' Meriden Co-operative, which had recently wrested control of the motorcycle manufacturer's Solihull factory, after a two year sit-in, from its private owners, Norton-Villiers-Triumph, a conglomerate of failed firms that had been cobbled together by the Government in a manner so characteristic of Britain's industrial ebb. On the inner sleeve, Burnel declared solidarity with the workers in a lusty, high-flown declamation:

THE TRIUMPH WORKERS' CO-OPERATIVE AT MERIDEN HAS PROVED THAT PERSONALLY MOTIVATED ENTERPRISE, COUPLED WITH GROUP INTEREST, IS A NECESSARY INGREDIENT IN SUCCESSFUL SOCIALISM AND THAT THE SHAM CALLED NATIONALISATION COULD ONLY BE SUGGESTED AND PERPETRATED BY ENEMIES OF THE PEOPLE.

The track itself was a towering instrumental built on the rhythm of Burnel's own Bonneville motorcycle ("Bonneville" being French for "Good city"), which necessitated its presence onstage when he toured the album with his own Euroband, resulting in consequent strife with bookers and local authorities. Its vertiginous muscularity is in telling contrast to The Human League's contemporaneous "Toyota City", which evokes a near-eternal oriental harmony. The British motorcycle industry had been, alongside shipbuilding, the home industry most chronically damaged by foreign competition, and this was largely because it had been vulnerable to a competitor more vigorous than even the reconstituted continental Europeans. Japan had in the post war years adopted a mercantilist export policy in which its banks had been financing indigenous industrial corporations at effectively negative interest rates, while these corporations themselves, having immersed themselves in the quality-first ethos of American production consultants such as W. Edwards Deming, had specifically aimed at eliminating external competitors through long-term plans which sometimes had an expected duration of 20 to 50 years.

Norton-Villiers-Triumph had been unable to compete with Japanese manufacturers in their crucial North American export market largely due to the high value of the pound, especially in comparison with the artificially devalued Japanese Yen. Even without this barrier, the Japanese would have been happy to sell their machines at a temporary loss purely to establish market dominance. As Burnel explained to the NME:

The Triumph Bonneville is basically a 30-year-old engine design. It's also one of the main reasons why the British motorbike industry disappeared: they weren't competing with the Japanese. But for some reason there were sufficient punters in the world who want something which is not sophisticated – I mean, you have to jump on it, you have to kick it over, you can't use a button to start it. And it vibrates like fuck. There is something intrinsically powerful and dignified about it.

Though an admirer of Japan for its resistance to American values, Burnel had a specifically European idea of what constituted an appropriate system of production, one that didn't fit with Japanese mass production philosophies. As he told Melody Maker:

Well look, the oldest form of private enterprise known to we Europeans is l'artisanat, or artisanship, which as far as I'm concerned is the only acceptable form of private enterprise. It's a group unit or team, not a syndicate or a large-scale corporation, it's very honest, sort of like the smithy down the road. L'artisanat is the intrinsic European way.

Burnel's conception of a distinctively European modernism was one that attempted to resolve the tension between technological advance and the sense of alienation that it so frequently evoked; he proposed a kind of warm-blooded, even gristly, modernism, which the sinewy "Triumph Of The Good City" successfully evoked. The throbbing, exposed cylinders of the Bonneville are writ large in the architectural form of the Centre Pompidou, which becomes a visceral machine for producing culture. Rather than being imported from some distant automated factory, untouched by human hands, industrial technology, downscaled to the co-operative group, once more becomes alive, perhaps in the same way it did to the Promethean engineers who foresaw, but didn't see the consequences of, the Industrial Revolution. Crucially though this vision had as its centre the idea of production being sufficiently personalised that it enhanced an individual's identity:

I think we should start looking to our roots. It's okay for black people to talk about their roots, but we Europeans have them, too. We have

roots in economic systems and we have much deeper cultural roots,
and we shouldn't be deferring to Washington, nor to Moscow either.

"Do The European" was another massive, muscular construction, the sound of a continent on the move. The lyrics focus on perhaps the greatest horror of identity – its sheer arbitrariness:

There are whites who'd rather be black
There are blacks who'd rather be white
There are always those who don't feel right
In their skins

Burnel recounts all the places he could have been born, all the people he could have been. And yet, there is only one identity he can submit to, the continent-spanning one that has roots in the ancient past and branches reaching out into the future. However, whereas "Toyota City" was inspired by the concrete phenomenon of a well-ordered Japanese industrial expansion, Burnel's vision was something of a chimera. Rather than an EEC composed of nation states, based around the necessities of finance and trade, he envisioned the very structure of Europe as being based around the primary requirement of granting a secure identity to all its inhabitants. As he told Chris Salewicz:

It's a very fundamental aspect of Europeanism. Imagine: in the United States of Europe there's no reason why Westminster should dictate to Scotland. When you hear these arseholes complaining that they'll lose their individuality it's always English people; people who've subjugated the Welsh for nine hundred years. There's no reason whatsoever why the English, whoever they are, should lose their identity at all.

Burnel's imagined mechanism for the emergence of this future United States of Europe was the sclerosis of the over-complexified bureaucratic structures through which the systems on both sides of the Iron Curtain operated:

> *I think that the giant corporate powers are going to start declining if for no other reason than they're dysfunctional. Also the whole monolith that we know at the moment as socialism is going to inevitably destroy itself because that's just a giant corporation also. Then we can have real socialism.*

Although Burnel claimed to reject the institution of the syndicate, his political ideas were essentially syndicalist. In an essay entitled "Systems" that he wrote for the NME in 1979 he referred to a mathematical concept known as the Sigmoid Curve, a function that charts the growth or progression of complex natural systems over time, and which demonstrates how such systems are inevitably bound to plateau (or "atrophy" in Burnel's own words). For Burnel, the looser, more flexible forms of syndicalist organi-sation were less prone to sclerosis than the monolithic structures of liberal capitalism or Soviet communism, and thus their eventual triumph could be guaranteed. However, both these systems, headquartered in Washington and Moscow, were still capable of stifling the emergence of his ideal Europe. Burnel's antipathy to the Soviet Union was every bit as intense as it was towards the USA. As he loftily proclaimed on the inner sleeve of the album:

> *A Europe riddled with American values and Soviet subversion is a diseased sycophantic old whore; a Europe strong, united and independent is a child of the future. The period of gestation has been long and painful. Euroman Cometh.*

If the song "Deutschland Nicht Uber Alles" chafed at the American "colonisation" of certain European nations, then "Euromess" raged against the repression that had become routine within the Warsaw Pact. It is almost an inversion of Suicide's

"Che", that band's requiem fugue for the Cuban revolutionary Che Guevara. "Euromess" documents the events of the Prague Spring a decade earlier when, on April the 5th 1968, the First Secretary of the Czechoslovak Communist Party Alexander Dubček published an "Action Programme" of "liberalisations", including the right to free speech and movement and a move toward greater political and economic autonomy from the Soviet Union. The subsequent Warsaw Pact invasion of Czechoslovakia saw the reversal of the reforms under a policy of "normalisation", and the arrest of many leading writers and dissidents. One such dissident, Jan Palach, set fire to himself in Wenceslas Square several months later in protest, not only at the invasion, but at the demoralisation within the population that it appeared to induce:

Don't forget how they liberalised
Then they normalised, they decivilised
Don't forget young Jan Palach
He burnt a torch against the Warsaw Pact

Nevertheless, as far as Burnel was concerned, the repression of the Soviet system, and the identity-corrosion inherent in the American version of liberal capitalism were the inevitably corrupt consequences of the sclerotic inefficiency induced by their over-complexity. As he explained to the NME:

Real socialism as portrayed by a workers' co-operative can't work outside of a capitalist society. I don't know if you've read any of the reports from the farm co-operatives in the Ukraine or in Georgia, but they're totally corrupt, mainly because of the high burden of obligation towards the central government: the characteristic Communist state, very centralised government. In order to institute that 150-year-old dogma i.e. nationalise all means of distribution and production – you have to have a centralised state. It's totally incongruous with what modern society should be aiming for.

Unfortunately, the Triumph Workers' Meriden Co-operative that was to trail blaze Burnel's new European paradigm went bankrupt and out of business in 1983, still struggling against the tide of a strong pound and an absence of investment capital, as well as facing a newly elected neo-liberal Conservative government that was ideologically opposed to the continued subsidy of "inefficient" industries. For all the syndicalist principles that had informed the creation of the Meriden Co-operative, it had still been reliant on state loans, most notably those granted by the Trade and Industry Secretary of the previous Labour Government, Tony Benn. The company would be bought and eventually resurrected by a conventional capitalist businessman, while the bureaucratization of Europe, even in the absence of the Warsaw Pact, would continue unabated.

In many ways, Burnel's lofty vision of a unified European continent providing a dignified home for latter day artisans was divorced from the urgent, and frequently grubby, street politics of the Britain of the late 1970s. The decade had witnessed the alarming rise of the far-Right, via the neo-fascist National Front with its broad approach of electoral politics and intimidatory marches, and the more directly violent and openly neo-Nazi British Movement. The initial impetus for the rise of the far-Right had been an incendiary speech given by the then Shadow Defence Secretary Enoch Powell at the Midland Hotel, Birmingham, on 20 April 1968, in which he recounted letters and conversational comments from anonymous constituents regarding immigrants from the British Commonwealth, one of whom remarked that *"in this country in 15 or 20 years' time the black man will have the whip hand over the white man."* Powell's speech, which was ostensibly a protest against the impending Race Relations Bill, called for the repatriation of non-white immigrants, and ended on an infamous reference to the Sybil prophecies in the *Aeneid*, in which *"like the Roman, I seem to see 'the River Tiber foaming with much blood'"*.

The National Front also advocated the repatriation of Commonwealth immigrants who had arrived under the British Nationality Act of 1948. Although the mid-seventies had seen its growth temporarily stall due to disputes between its overtly nationalist and neo-Nazi leadership factions, by 1974 it had 50 branches throughout Britain, and an estimated membership of up to 20,000. In 1973 its candidate for the West Bromwich West by-election had polled just over 16% of the vote, a result that had alarmed the political and media establishment. If anti-immigration sentiment and neo-fascist apologetics were beginning to make inroads into mainstream politics, they were also encroaching on the music scene. After The Beatles and Roger Daltrey of The Who had made some indignant comments about immigration, Rod Stewart was to tell the International Times in 1970 *"I think Enoch is the man. I'm all for him. This country is overcrowded. The immigrants should be sent home. That's it."* Stewart's comments weren't widely publicised, but comments made by a drunken Eric Clapton during a concert at the Odeon in Birmingham (on the same street where Powell had conjured the "Rivers Of Blood") in August 1976 provoked consternation. Clapton entreated his audience:

> *I think we should vote for Enoch Powell. Enoch's our man. I think Enoch's right. I think we should send them all back. Stop Britain from becoming a black colony. Get the foreigners out, get the wogs out, get the coons out. Keep Britain white. I used to be into dope, but now I'm into racism. It's much heavier, man … we are a white country, I don't want fucking wogs living next to me with their standards.*

The National Front's notion of "keeping Britain white" was very redolent of the "Keep Britain Tidy" anti-litter campaigns of the era, the intimation being that Commonwealth migrants were some kind of refuse that needed to be deposited elsewhere. But it was the sheer gall of a man who had built his career on the appropriation of African-American and Jamaican music wanting to pull up the ethnic shutters that catalysed a reaction. This reaction was initiated by Red Saunders, a portrait photographer and political activist, who with his friend Roger Huddle and the performance group Kartoon Klowns sent a letter to the NME, Melody Maker, Sounds and the Socialist Worker admonishing Clapton with the reminder that *"Half your music is black. You're rock's biggest colonist … Who shot the Sheriff, Eric? It sure as hell wasn't you!"* Huddle appealed to the papers' readerships *"to organise a rank and file movement against the racist poison music. We urge support for Rock Against Racism."*

This request garnered several hundred immediate replies, though the sense of urgency was intensified the following month when a drug-addled David Bowie gave an interview to Playboy in which he described Adolf Hitler as *"one of the first rock stars"* and opined that *"Britain could benefit from a fascist leader"* in order to *"sweep everything off its feet and tidy everything up."* This "tidying up" was proving lethal to anyone who opposed it or was targeted by it. Kevin Gately had been killed, probably by a mounted policeman, at an anti-fascist rally in Red Lion Square in June 1974. When Gurdip Singh Chaggar, an Asian teenager, was murdered by a white gang in Southall, John Kingsley Read of the National Front had announced *"one down, a million to go!"* Rock Against Racism held its first gig in a pub in East London in November 1976, and from then on mushroomed into a nationwide organisation, with its own fanzine, *Temporary Hoarding*, whose first editorial stated:

> *We want Rebel music, street music, music that breaks down people's fear of one another. Crisis music. Now music. Music that knows who the real enemy is. Rock Against Racism. Love Music Hate Racism.*

The movement started to attract many of the upcoming names in the punk subculture, notably The Clash, the Tom Robinson Band,

X-Ray Spex and Sham 69, as well as reggae acts such as Steel Pulse and Misty In Roots. It was vital to Rock Against Racism to bring white and black performers together as a symbol of racial harmony. In addition to catalysing the energy of the punk scene, RAR provided a locus for other initiatives on the radical Left. The Anti-Nazi League was formed in 1977 as a front of the Socialist Workers Party, the newly-minted name of the International Socialists, and ran leafleting campaigns and organised direct actions against the National Front and British Movement, similar to the harassment of the NF rally at Green Lanes in April of that year.

The opposition to the National Front was starting to co-ordinate itself effectively just as the Front itself was creating an electoral toehold; the elections to the Greater London Council in May 1977 had put them in fourth place, albeit with only 5% of the vote. Both the ANL and RAR responded to this by co-ordinating a joint demonstration and concert in London's Victoria Park to encourage the youth vote against the NF in the local council elections the following spring. The concert, in April 1978, featured a memorable performance by The Clash, the earnestness of which would provide a striking contrast to the equally indelible, stripper-festooned show that The Stranglers would mount at Battersea Park later in the year.

As if on cue, support for the National Front crumbled at the local elections, and even more so at the General Election the following year, in which the party only gained 0.6% of the vote. And yet the effectiveness of Rock Against Racism, and indeed the commitment of the punk movement toward supporting it are open to conjecture. As Roger Sabin has pointed out, some punk bands such as The Vibrators and The Art Attacks performed RAR gigs purely for careerist reasons, or for the fact that the gigs were well paid, and included full expenses. There were bands who were openly hostile to ANL/RAR such as Alternative TV, whose singer Mark Perry stated:

RAR preach against the NF but on their badge is the red star, which has caused as much trouble and animosity as the swastika. I don't need to be told by a commie organisation to love blacks ... the SWP and NF are as bad as each other.

There was a general suspicion of RAR within the punk movement; that it was middle-class, that it was hippie (which its fondness for festivals seemed to confirm), that it was as much a tool of manipulative ideologues as the NF's attempts to infiltrate the punk scene. Most pertinently, as Sabin also describes, there were stylistic elements within the very core of punk that really were politically dubious – the wearing of swastikas; lyrics that castigated or mocked Jews, Arabs, Hispanics; aesthetic and lyrical appreciations of the Third Reich; the ambivalent use of the Union Jack. These are nowadays written off as being symptomatic of a general urge to shock, but as Sabin notes, this may just be a convenient excuse that allows racism to be "edited out" of the punk story to conform to an anti-racist myth.

Another element that informed attitudes towards RAR was the simple dog-eat-dog competitiveness within the punk scene. In many ways, Rock Against Racism appealed to those punk bands that were the most earnest, and therefore often the most musically pedestrian. Certainly it was the more avant-garde or outspoken bands that tended to either mock it or only give it lip service. Neither The Sex Pistols nor Public Image Limited played gigs for RAR, despite John Lydon's vocal hostility towards the National Front. Rock Against Racism was almost tailor-made for the weak socialist humanism of a band like The Clash, who hankered for a better world, but many punks had no such yearnings.

Rock Against Racism was problematic for The Stranglers in a number of ways. Firstly, and most obviously, they felt no compulsion to pretend to join together in one big family with a punk scene that had spent the previous couple of years venomously rejecting them. Secondly, the connection between RAR and the Anti-Nazi League was unacceptable to Burnel for two reasons. The first one was that he had been the subject of some hostile press from the NME's two SWP-aligned correspondents, Tony Parsons and Julie Burchill. Parsons had followed The Stranglers and the Finchley Boys on tour in 1977, and had suggested Burnel was a homosexual and a Nazi; the latter charge at least Burnel considered to be slanderous. The second one was that Burnel was opposed to the SWP politically. As he was to later tell Paul Marko of Punk77.com:

> *The fascist thing came about because everyone must be a fascist who doesn't want to join the Socialist Worker Party. Because Tony Parsons and Julie Burchill were SWP they had that as part of their agenda. I didn't agree with it or with RAR. Rough Trade refused to stock our records because of this. Just because you have your own opinion. We weren't going to jump on any political bandwagon. Dave, Hugh and Jet thought it was really stupid. The world isn't like that, it's more subtle. We refused to do RAR.*

In fact, Burnel levelled a familiar charge against the radical Left; that its relationship with fascism was libidinal; that it had to accentuate the threat that the National Front posed in order to exaggerate its own role in opposing it. He gave a rather bizarre analogy to Chris Salewicz of the NME:

> *The National Front doesn't really exist. They got about 0.2 per cent of the votes at the last by-elections. They're being used by the SWP in the same way that extremists always create myths to hate. Like Hitler made the Jews an object of hatred, for example.*

Nevertheless, the band felt they had to take their own stance against racism, and their vehicle for this was a joint headline tour with the Birmingham-based reggae band Steel Pulse, who were at the time one of the very few groups of any kind who were prepared to be associated with The Men In Black. As Burnel would tell Paul Marko:

We went on tour with the reggae band Steel Pulse who played with a strong political message. When they played the Midlands, I think Wolverhampton where they were from, they were getting bottles thrown at them and all types of abuse from a white Stranglers audience – our audience – and they didn't know what to do. We were so embarrassed that we walked on stage and apologized. Jet made a speech: 'These are our friends and if you don't have the intelligence to respect their 45 minute set then you have no respect for us. If you have a problem we will be waiting by the side for you.' Silence. And everybody listened to the set. The band who weren't sure about white people got to know us as friends. That said more about RAR bullshit.

Although the two bands might at first appear to be an awkward pairing, they had much in common. Both bands considered themselves to be in Babylon, although The Stranglers' conception had an idiosyncratic extraterrestrial component. Also, The Stranglers' sound was deeply reggae influenced, a characteristic that had originated during their early period in Chiddingford, when they hired out their PA system to dub and toasting nights at Acton Town Hall for pin money. The dominant sound of the bass speakers at these events, together with the delayed snare, made a deep impression on Burnel, and from then on the band attempted to incorporate them into their music.

The final reason Burnel opposed the SWP/RAR agenda was because he attached a great deal of importance to the notion of a deeply-rooted identity. As he told Phil McNeill:

I resent the SWP and all Moscow lovers and Washington lovers. I don't see anything wrong in finding and digging the best things from one's own roots, which is why I consider myself to be a European.

As far as he was concerned, no ideological vision could substitute for a sense of belonging, and in a strange way, the rock aristocrats whose offensive outbursts had inspired Rock Against Racism go some way to demonstrating that. Eric Clapton was the bastard son of a Canadian soldier who Clapton himself had never set eyes on. Rod Stewart had spent his career not really convincing anyone that he was a Scotsman like his father. The half-Irish David Bowie was at the time impersonating a decaying English aristocrat, the Thin White Duke, and he wasn't going to be the last Anglo-Irish pop performer who would dabble with the far-Right. Although the radical Left tends to frame racism as a kind of disease of thought that is susceptible to ideological amelioration in the great sweep of social progress, it may in many cases simply be the process in which those with a marginal identity shore up their claims to inclusion by pointing out those who are visibly more marginal still. Certainly this would explain why Nicky Crane was at this time harassing Rock Against Racism concerts on behalf of the British Movement.

Rock Against Racism and the Anti-Nazi League quickly fell into abeyance after the 1979 General Election and the decline of the National Front. Margaret Thatcher had moved the Conservative Party further to the Right, and her interview with ITV's "World In Action" television programme, in which she observed that the British public were *"afraid that this country might be rather swamped by people with a different culture"* and that *"we are a British nation with British characteristics"*, had been effective in luring the NF's Tory sympathisers back into the fold. Nonetheless, Rock Against Racism and Anti-Nazi League activists considered that they had performed a crucial role in demonstrating to the National Front that they could mobilize the nation's youth far more effectively than any far-Right movement could. Certainly most of the movement's black and Asian supporters concurred with that assessment.

If *Euroman Cometh* had been mostly preoccupied with the

weighty subject of the political destiny of a continent, there was still room for some chauvinist filth, most notably with the venereal jauntiness of "Crabs", and "Pretty Face", a cover of a song by the Sixties R&B group The Beat Merchants. Burnel amended the lyrics to once more exercise his masculine-protest superiority complex:

Your big brown eyes are for looking at me
Your lips are for kissing my feet
Your little hands are for my special parts
I've found a lover

But the effect was considerably diminished in comparison to "Death And Night And Blood", as any lingering sense of inferiority was being abreacted by his increasingly coherent European identity, which subsumed the contradictions between his British and French identities within a greater whole. Although known by the rest of the band as "John" it had been the record company that had insisted on him using his real name, to lend the group an air of exoticism. Both the continentalism of his Europhilia, and his advocacy of regional identity were ways of averting the commitment to choose between two personas that were difficult to resolve in a single individual. As Jet Black was to tell the Burning Up Times:

Well I think he's always been a bit schizoid ... I don't know what
that is, but it might simply be the deep influence of French culture
on his psyche, and as you know, the French do and think the
complete opposite of Brits, so I think unbeknown to him he has this
kind of schism in his personality when one day he's wearing a beret,
and the next day he's wearing a trilby...

The first indication that Burnel was starting to resolve this schism came with the title track of The Stranglers' *La Folie* album in 1981.

The inspiration for the song came from a particularly gruesome murder that had been enacted in Paris earlier that year. Issei Sagawa, a Japanese student of French Literature at the Sorbonne, had killed a beautiful Dutch fellow student, Renée Hartevelt, and then had sex with her corpse, before dismembering parts of it to eat. When caught attempting to dump the mutilated remains, he explained to the French police that he not unreasonably felt himself to be a *"weak, ugly, and small man"*, and had hoped to acquire some of Hartevelt's health and beauty by consuming her flesh.

It is not difficult to understand why Burnel found the story so intriguing. Cannibalism was a perennial obsession of The Stranglers, and here was an example of masculine protest taken to its ultimate conclusion; the literal acting out of the need to internally consume the weak, "inferior" feminine side of the self to create a coherent whole. Sagawa's act was a corrupted attempt at magic; a sick alchemy. Significantly, Sagawa was Japanese, and it was through the Japanese martial art of Shidokan karate that Burnel had imposed self-discipline and focus on himself in order to control his internal conflicts.

That the murder had happened in France was also significant, and the song was sung, or rather narrated, in French, which allowed Burnel to express a side of himself that had hitherto remained suppressed within the oeuvre of the band. Rather than revel in the horror of the murder, "La Folie" expresses a world-weary regret; that we all carry something of the emptiness that motivated Sagawa; that we are all capable of a portion of his madness. As Burnel put it, *"even God has deserted us"*.

There once was a student
Who had a great desire, as they say in books
His girlfriend was so sweet that by eating her,
He was able to reject all vices, repulse all evil
Destroy everything beautiful

Which up until then, had never been known to him
Because he was mad, yes it is madness
(trans.)

The following year, Burnel successfully lobbied for the song to be released as a single in the wake of the success of "Golden Brown", much to the chagrin of Cornwell, and its failure to enter the UK Top 40 prompted significant disquiet within the band. Cornwell, chastened after his experiences in prison, felt that an opportunity to regain career momentum had been lost, but this was somewhat churlish as there is no doubt that "La Folie" is one of the very greatest songs that The Stranglers recorded, and, in the chaotic pop world that followed the eruption of punk, it was by no means impossible that even something as bold as this could chart, if a few radio producers had been willing to give it air time.

"La Folie" was sonically reminiscent of *Seppuku*, the grimy, brooding album Burnel had produced for the Parisian group Taxi Girl. With song titles such as "Avenue Du Crime" and "Les Armées de la Nuit", and its cover of a geisha preparing herself for ritual suicide, the record seemed to be channeling The Stranglers' darkest compulsions. The Japanese practice of seppuku, or honour suicide, had long been of interest to Burnel, and in a strange way it echoed Sagawa's deviancy in that, in the opinion of the sociologist Emile Durkheim, suicide too could be counted as a magical act; a means of resolving social contradictions. Durkheim viewed suicide as a solution to the problem of the existence of the individual, and the terrible sense of "sticking out" from the "social chorus" that every individual person experiences, especially when indulging in the "barely acceptable" behaviour of spontaneity. Durkheim believed that all suicide was, to some degree, a socially-induced means of death, in which an individual succumbs to external pressure through such mechanisms as shame, disapproval or neglect. An "archaic" form of suicide such as seppuku, the preserve of warrior castes, on the other hand served as a method of resolving the social contradiction of the individual by allowing a return to *koinonia*, or communion with the social whole, without compromising the individual's honour.

However, it was to be a single released at the end of the year that was to demonstrate that Burnel could write a Top Ten hit, and was also to reveal that he had succeeded in the magical process of individuation. "European Female" was as sublime, and as significant to its author, as "Golden Brown" was to Cornwell. A paean to the goddess Europa, it is the sound of Burnel subsuming his muse; the "European female" affirms his pan-continental identity and marks the apex of his creative arc. The masculine, English, motorcycle-riding John is resolved with the weak, French, feminine Jean Jacques. The chiliasm of the lyrics is no exaggeration, as the man whose family roots are buried in Calvados was to tell Gary Kent many years later:

Now I call myself English, Norman English. The Normans and us have had a relationship for a thousand years and I'd like to keep it going.

zer0
books

Contemporary culture has eliminated both the concept of the public and the figure of the intellectual. Former public spaces – both physical and cultural – are now either derelict or colonized by advertising. A cretinous anti-intellectualism presides, cheered by expensively educated hacks in the pay of multinational corporations who reassure their bored readers that there is no need to rouse themselves from their interpassive stupor. The informal censorship internalized and propagated by the cultural workers of late capitalism generates a banal conformity that the propaganda chiefs of Stalinism could only ever have dreamt of imposing. Zer0 Books knows that another kind of discourse – intellectual without being academic, popular without being populist – is not only possible: it is already flourishing, in the regions beyond the striplit malls of so-called mass media and the neurotically bureaucratic halls of the academy. Zer0 is committed to the idea of publishing as a making public of the intellectual. It is convinced that in the unthinking, blandly consensual culture in which we live, critical and engaged theoretical reflection is more important than ever before.